Press Law in Nigeria

Malthouse Law Books

Adah C. E., *The Nigerian Law of Evidence*

Egweike, K., *Nigerian Commercial Law: Agency*

Egweike, K., *Nigerian Commercial Law: Hire Purchase*

Egweike, K., *Nigerian Commercial Law: Contract*

Fogam, P., *Law of Contract*

Sagay, I., *Family Law in Nigeria*

Shoyele O., *Principles and Practice of Administrative Law in Nigeria*

Uvieghara E. E., *Labour Law in Nigeria*

Yakubu J. A., *Limits to the Application of Foreign Laws*

Yakubu J. A., *International Contracts: Evolution and Theory*

Yakubu J. A.,(ed.) *Administration of Justice in Nigeria*

Yakubu J. A. & Oyewo, A. T., *Criminal Law & Procedure in Nigeria*

Press Law in Nigeria

by

Dr. John Ademola Yakubu
LL.B (Hons); B.L.; LL.M; Ph.D.
Reader, Faculty of Law,
University of Ibadan, Ibadan, Nigeria.
&
formerly Honourable Attorney General and
Commissioner for Justice,
Oyo State of Nigeria.

MALTHOUSE PRESS LTD
Lagos, Benin, Ibadan, Jos, Oxford

Malthouse Press Limited
8, Amore Street, Off Toyin Street, Ikeja,
P.O. Box 500, Ikeja, Lagos State, Nigeria.

Lagos, Benin, Ibadan, Jos, Oxford, Port-Harcourt, Zaria

© John Ademola Yakubu 1999
First published 1999
ISBN 978 023 098 X

Dedication

This book is dedicated to Morse, Peter, Lynne, Michael and Phillippa Spencer.

Acknowledgements

I am grateful to God who has made it possible for this work to be completed. I am grateful to Prof. Mrs. Abiola Odejide under whose tenure as Head of Department of Communication Arts, University of Ibadan, Ibadan, I taught Press Law (post Graduate) and Legal Aspect of Communication (Undergraduate) in the Department. I must also express my appreciation to other members of staff of the Department of Communication Arts especially Dr. E. O. Soola and Dr. J. O. Akinleye for their cooperation. The incisive criticisms, questions and comments of the students have gone a long way in enriching this book.

I am grateful to Prof. J. D. Ojo, the Dean of the Faculty of Law of the University of Ibadan, Ibadan for writing the foreword to this book. He made useful texts and journals available to me. He also read through the manuscript. He has done much to enrich this work. I thank Prof. Omoniyi Adewoye, the Vice Chancellor of the University of Ibadan, Ibadan for his encouragement.

I must also mention the name of Chief Akin Olujinmi, SAN who read the manuscript and made very useful comments. He provided me with essential cases on the chapters contained in this book. I am indeed very grateful to him.

It is imperative for me to mention the name of Dr. A.T. Oyewo. He spurred me into action. At the time I was reluctant to put my pen on paper, he literally forced my hand to hold the biro and at the time I wanted to sleep for hours, he drummed into my ears the futility of leaving my potentials locked up in my brain. I thank all the members of staff of the Ministry of Justice for making it possible for me to achieve success as the Honourable Attorney-General and Commissioner for Justice of the State. I am grateful to Mr 'Niyi Otunla, Honourable Justice K. Ariwoola and Wole Oladokun for their care. I thank my junior ones for their care and support. It is my hope that this work will be of immense benefit to all who cherish freedom of expression and the Press. Perhaps this book attests to the truth of the comment made by Navy Captain Anthony Ibe Onyearugbulem, the Military Administrator of Edo State who once referred to me as "the good boy of the Press".

Dr. John Ademola Yakubu,
Faculty of Law,
University of Ibadan,
Ibadan.
14 July, 1999.

Foreword

Dr Yakubu's work on *Press Law in Nigeria* is of great interest. He has approached the work as a lawyer not as a political scientist nor as a historian. He has examined in detail several provisions on Press Law in Nigeria and has written a good critique of them. His language is very simple and lucid. His analysis is very critical and penetrating. Any one looking at the work would find it to be a product of a sound scholar and a very good researcher. There is no doubt that this work will make a useful addition to the works in this field. This is why I am recommending it to every student of law, the Bar, the Bench and those interested in the development of the law in this area will find the work a *sine qua non*.

Professor J. D. Ojo
Dean, Faculty of Law
University of Ibadan
9 July, 1999

Preface

One of the cherished tenets is that relating to freedom of expression and the Press. So fundamental is the idea of freedom that when a person's freedom is unjustifiably taken away, the law deems it fit that compensation be paid to him. This idea has been given a pride of place in the various Nigerian Constitutions. Of particular consideration in this book is the 1979 Constitution. The 1999 Constitution is mainly an amendment of the 1979 Constitution. It is therefore safe to base our discussion on the 1979 Constitution. This could be used as a guide in the interpretation of the provisions of the 1999 Constitution. Furthermore, the 1979 Constitution has developed its own jurisprudence since our courts have decided on many of its provisions. Indeed, the idea of freedom of the Press is recognised universally. Provisions relating to Press freedom can be found in the Constitutions of countries like India and the United States of America among others. The African Charter of Human and People's Rights contains provisions relating to freedom of expression and the Press.

It is imperative that a journalist knows how he stands with the law in the effort to keep the public informed of events or issues of national or international importance. Except this is appreciated, confinement, loss of revenue through payment of damages and loss of credibility may be the lot of many Newspaper Houses and Journalists. Omo Bedu writing in *The Nigerian Sunday Sketch* of March 31, 1974 at page 6, Ojo (1976) had this to say under the caption - "Hazards and Joys of the Press".

> Like any other job, journalism has its joy and
> sorrows. There is no other group of people who have
> chats with the Police more frequently than the
> journalists. When the police really gets agitated, hair
> shaving and whipping can go with the chat. It is also
> true that the journalist runs the risk of standing trial
> for libel, sedition and similar offences. So the job of
> a journalist has its hazards.

The thorny issue in relation to the scope of freedom of expression and the Press has been discussed especially under the 1979 Constitution. The controversial issue whether a journalist must disclose his source of information has been comprehensively discussed. An attempt has also been made to show the requirements of good legal writing. The offences which a journalist may run foul of and the defences available to a journalist when any of the offences is committed is also discussed. In essence, this book is a necessary companion for journalists, Mass Communication students, Lawyers, Judges and anyone who has something to do with the Press or who is interested in freedom of expression and the Press.

Dr John Ademola Yakubu
Faculty of Law,
University of Ibadan,
Ibadan,
14 July, 1999

Contents

Table of cases

Table of statutes

1

The press under the constitution

The press, usually referred to as the fourth estate of the realm has a vital role to play not only in relation to information dissemination but also in nation building. The extent to which the press of a nation can go in achieving its noble objective depends on each society. So fundamental is the role of the press that a place has been found for it in the Nigerian Constitution.[1]

Section 36 of the 1979 Constitution tagged "Right to freedom of expression and the press" provides:

> (1) every person shall be entitled to freedom of expression, including freedom to hold opinions and to receive and impart ideas and information without interference.
>
> (2) Without prejudice to the generality of subsection (1) of this section, every person shall be entitled to own, establish and operate any medium for the dissemination of information, ideas and opinions: provided that no person, other than the Government of the Federation or of a State or any other person or body authorised by the President, shall own, establish or operate a television or wireless broadcasting station for any purpose whatsoever.
>
> (3) Nothing in this section shall invalidate any law that is reasonably justifiable in a democratic society...
>
> (a) for the purpose of preventing the disclosure of information received in confidence, maintaining the

---

[1] See also Article 125 of the Soviet Union's 1936 (Stalin) Constitution.

authority and independence of courts or regulating telephony, wireless broadcasting, television or the exhibition of cinematography films; or

(b) imposing restrictions upon persons holding office under the Government of the Federation or of a state, members of the Armed Forces of the Federation or members of the Nigeria Police Force.

Section 21 of the 1979 Constitution also provides that

the press, radio, television and other agencies of the mass media shall at all times be free to uphold the fundamental objectives contained in this chapter and uphold the responsibility and accountability of the Government to the people.

Analysis of the constitutional provisions

Section 36 of the 1979 Constitution guarantees freedom of speech as well as freedom to hold opinions. It also gives each person the right to be educated and to educate others and impart ideas and information without interference, censor or inhibition.

This provision is in line with the universal conception that freedom of the press and freedom of expression are so fundamental that any law that tends to obstruct any of the two ideas cannot be law properly so called. Blackstone had this view in focus when he opined that the "the liberty of the press is indeed essential to the nature of a free state." He went further to state that "every free man has an undoubted right to lay what sentiments he pleases before the public; to forbid this, is to destroy the freedom of the press."[2]

---

[2] Blackstone *Commentaries on the Laws of England*

In the same vein, Article 19 of the Universal Declaration of Human Rights states that:

> everyone has the right to freedom of opinion and expression. The right includes freedom to hold opinion without interference and to seek, receive and impart information and ideas through any media and regardless of frontiers.[3]

The cumulative effect of these provisions is that it is fundamental in any civilised society to guarantee the right of each person to express himself not only in respect of issues or matters of individual nature but also in respect of issues of public interest. Since man is a political animal, he would necessarily be interested in the events that happen around him and if he is so interested, he has the right to inform others or the public at large. Furthermore, modern system, modern ideas and indeed the improvement in global communication system now make communication possible not only in respect of *inter partes* communication but also in respect of communication with any person who may be thousands of kilometres away. The importance of this constitutional provision cannot therefore be over-emphasised. Indeed to be informed is to be educated.

Before a detailed analysis of the provision of section 36 is discussed any further, it is necessary to determine the meaning of the two expressions, "freedom of expression" and "freedom of the press". Freedom according to the *New Lexicon of Webster's Dictionary*, relates to enjoyment of personal liberty, of not being a slave nor a prisoner. Freedom of expression therefore relates to the liberty of open discussion without fear of restriction or restraint. Freedom of the press has acquired a

---

[3] See also Article 125 of the Soviet Union's 1936 (Stalin) Constitution

technical meaning. According to Blackstone, it consists in laying no previous restraints upon publication, and not in freedom from censure for criminal matter when published. He went further:

> every free man has an undoubted right to lay what sentiments he pleases before the public; to forbid this, is to destroy the freedom of the press.

He also adumbrated what will be discussed later in respect of the limit to this freedom. According to him:

> to publish, as the law does...any dangerous or offensive writings, which when published, shall on a fair and impartial trial be adjudged of a pernicious tendency, is necessary for the preservation of peace and good order of government and religion, the only solid foundation of civil society.

This provision is not confined to the press as it talks of "every person." Thus anyone, not only citizens of Nigeria but aliens alike have the right to express themselves without any interference or censure subject only to the provisions of the Constitution for the protection of all. The fact that the expression applies to all is justified by the constitution. Although it starts with "we the People of the Federal Republic of Nigeria" yet, it goes further to state:

> having firmly and solemnly resolved to provide for a constitution for the purpose of promoting the good governance and welfare of all persons in our country on the principles of Freedom, Equality and Justice, and for the purpose of consolidating the unity of our people...do hereby make, enact and give to ourselves the following constitution.

The welfare of all persons in the country can only be ensured if uninhibited discussion is ensured and encouraged. The idea is strengthened by the provision of the United Nations Declaration of Human Rights that guarantees everyone the right to freedom of opinion and expression.

The freedom under consideration includes freedom to hold opinions. As human beings, the freedom to hold to one's belief is fundamental. This is because each person has the right to have a perspective of the world, the circumstances around him and the people he interacts with. He has the right to draw conclusions one way or the other and ordinarily this idea should not be stultified. He also has the right to educate himself as well as others and to keep them informed without any hindrance. The issue here has been given focus by the network of the media, schools, churches, political associations and organizations that try to educate and inform people both privately and publicly. Of course, the idea of educating and imparting knowledge and information starts from home.

Apart from section 36 of the Constitution, section 21 of the 1979 Constitution also deals with the mass media. The section is titled "obligations of the mass media". It states:

> The press, radio, television and other agencies of the mass media shall at all times be free to uphold the fundamental objectives contained in this chapter and uphold the responsibility and accountability of the government to the people.

It should be noted that much as this provision ensures or enhances freedom of the press, non-observance of it, on the basis of this provision alone is not justifiable in a court of law. What is meant by this is that chapter II of the Constitution which deals with Fundamental Objectives and Directive Principles of

State Policy makes provisions for political objectives which the government in power must observe. The non-observance of these provisions cannot be questioned in a court of law. Put in another way, the Directive Principles stated in the Constitution are policies which are expected to be pursued in the effort of the nation to realise national ideals.[4] It should also be pointed out that these provisions are the beacon to guide the Government in steering the ship of the state.

In the Indian case of *State of Madras* v *Champakan Dorairajin*,[5] the court was faced with the interpretation of a provision in the Indian Constitution which was similar to the provision of fundamental objectives in the Nigerian Constitution. The supreme court of India held:

> the directive principles of the state policy which by Article 37 expressly made unenforceable by a court cannot override the provisions found in part III which notwithstanding other provisions, are expressly made unenforceable by appropriate writs, orders or directives under Article 32. The chapter of Fundamental Rights is sacrosanct and cannot be abridged by any legislative or executive act or order, except to the extent provided in the appropriate Articles in Part III. The Directive Principles... have to conform to and run as subsidiary to the chapter of fundamental rights.

This was also the view of the Lagos High Court in *Archbishop A.O. Okogie* v *A.G. (Lagos State)*.[6] The court held that the Directive Principles of State Policy in Chapter II of the 1979 Constitution have to conform to and run as subsidiary to the Fundamental Rights under chapter IV of the Constitution.

---

[4] This was the view of the Constitutional Drafting Committee (Vol. 1 p.v).

[5] (1951) AIR S.C. 226

[6] (1981) N.C.L.R, 218

Also in *Hon. Attorney-General Borno State Ors.* v *Rev J.J. Adamu & Ors*,[7] the court held that by virtue of section 6(6)(c) of the 1979 Constitution, the determination of whether or not any authority or person is in breach of the provisions under chapter II of the 1979 Constitution has been excluded.

The implication of this is that any person aggrieved by non-observance of any of the provisions relating to Fundamental Objectives and Directive Principles of State Policy cannot go to a court of law for the determination of this issue as to achieve the objective of having the judgment of the court in this regard enforced as any other issue of a general nature can be enforced. Interestingly, section 6(6)(c) of the 1979 constitution takes out the Fundamental Objectives issue out of the jurisdiction of the court. It states:

> The judicial powers vested in accordance with the foregoing provisions of this section shall not, except as otherwise provided in this constitution, extend to any issue or question as to whether any act or omission by any authority or person or as to whether any law or any judicial decision is in conformity with the Fundamental Objectives and Directive Principles of State policy set out in chapter II of this constitution.

This provision therefore qualifies section 6(6)(a) which states that the judicial powers vested in accordance with the foregoing provisions of this section shall extend, notwithstanding anything to the contrary in this constitution, to all inherent powers and sanctions of a court of law.

---

[7] (1996) 1 NWLR (pt 427) 681.

It should also be noted that the operation of section 36 of the 1979 Constitution like other provisions on Fundamental Human Rights has been curtailed by section 41. It states:

> Nothing in sections 34, 35, 36, 37, and 38 of this constitution shall invalidate any law that is reasonably justifiable in a democratic society;
> (a) in the interest of defence, public safety, public order, public morality or public health, or
> for the purpose of protecting the rights and freedom of other persons.

The implication of this is that section 41 expressly permits derogation from the guaranteed rights provided in the sections relating to fundamental human rights. It is therefore certain that on account of defence, public safety, public order, public morality or public health, the right or freedom guaranteed under the constitution can be disregarded.   This section however states that the law invalidating the rights so guaranteed should be "reasonably justifiable in a democratic society." It needs to be determined (a) when is a law reasonably justifiable and (b)what is meant by a democratic society.

The meaning of the expression "reasonably justifiable" was considered in *Olawoyin* v *Attorney-General of Northern Nigeria*,[8] Bate J. called in aid the meaning given to a similar expression in India and the United States of America and came to the following conclusion:

> (I) The presumption that the legislature has acted constitutionally and that the laws which they passed are necessary and reasonable;

---

[8] (1961) 1 All NLR 269

(II) a restriction upon a fundamental human right before it
   may be considered justifiable must;
   (a)   be necessary in the interest of public morality or
   public order and
   (b)   not be excessive or out of proportion to the object
   which it is sought to achieve.

Apart from the above, the idea whether a particular act is
reasonably justifiable has been given meaning by the
constitution itself. For the act to be justifiable, it must be so in a
democratic society and by virtue of section 41(2) any measure
taken in accordance with the exigency of the situation especially
during a period of emergency can also be excused given the
above provision.

The determination of whether a particular act is justifiable in
a democratic society is a question of fact to be determined by
the facts presented before the court. In *Chief S. L. Akintola* v *Sir
Adesoji Aderemi & Ors*[9] Ademola CJF held:

> Ours is a constitutional democracy. It is of the essence of
> democracy that all its members are imbued with a spirit of
> tolerance, compromise and restraint. Those in power are
> willing to respect the fundamental rights of everyone,
> including the minority; and the minority will not be over-
> obstructive towards the majority. Both sides will observe the
> principles as accepted principles in a democratic society.

It seems that the purport of this provision is a call for the
observance of the rule of law. This perhaps was what operated in
the mind of the judge in *Re Mohammed Olayori*[10] when he held:

---

[9] (1962) WNLR 185.
[10] Suit No. M/196/69 of 17/11/69.

I am, as I know is every member of the Bench and every
right thinking and honest member of our society, against
prevailing conditions of corruption and embezzlement of
public funds existing in the country (Nigeria) today, but if
we are to live by the rule of law; if we are to have our
actions guided and restrained in certain ways for the benefit
of the society in general individual members in particular,
then whatever status, whatever post we hold we must
succumb to the rule of law. The alternative is anarchy and
chaos, and the whole purport of the Defence Regulation and
Emergency Regulations is to prevent this state of things.

This was the essence of the decision of the court in *Amakiri v
Iwowari,*[11] Miner Amakiri was a chief correspondent of the
Nigerian Observer in Rivers State. He was detained on July 30,
1974 for twenty-seven hours. His head was shaved and he was
given twenty-four strokes of the cane. His alleged offence was
based on his report on the threat issued by the chairman of the
Rivers State wing of the Nigerian Union of Teachers. He
reported that the attitude of the Ministry of Education to this
demand was nonchalant. On being asked why the journalist was
detained, his "offence" was said to the based on the publication
of that story which was said to have embarrassed the
government and particularly because it was published on the
Governor's birthday. He later sued for unlawful detention,
assault and battery. Amakiri was awarded ₦200 for each of the
twenty-four strokes of the cane. Further damages were awarded
for false imprisonment and shaving of his hair.

In a democratic set-up, the constitution normally states the
rules and procedure for governance and for orderly change by
election. A widely known feature of our political organisation is
that military rule seems to be the order of the day. This is

---

[11] Unreported.

because military rule has taken the better part of political governance in Nigeria since independence.

A usual feature is the suspension of the various constitutions upon ascendance to power by the Military through the fiat of what has always been known as Decree No. 1. A common feature of the intendment of such Decrees can be determined from section 4 of Decree No. 2 of 1984. It states: "No suit or other legal proceedings shall lie against any person for anything done or intended to be done in pursuance of this Act."

It further states that:

> Chapter IV of the constitution of the Federal Republic of Nigeria is hereby suspended for the purpose of this Act and any question whether any provision thereof has been or is being or would be contravened by anything done or purported to be done in pursuance of this Act shall not be inquired into in any court of law...[12]

One may ask, what has been the reaction of the courts having regard to the draconian effect of decrees like the one just cited. The position of the Nigerian courts is typified by the decision of the court of Appeal in *Wang Ching Yao &Ors* v *Chief of Staff Supreme Headquarters & Ors*.[13] The court held:

> the combined effect of the provisions of Decree No. 2 and Decree No. 13 of 1984 is that on the question of civil liberties, the law courts of Nigeria must...now blow muted trumpets.

This is an unfortunate development. It is now necessary to consider section 41 of the Constitution which is titled

---

[12] This is the chapter relating to Fundamental Human Rights
[13] CA/L/25/85.

"Restriction of Rights". The basis of this provision is the felt need to emphasise that though some rights are fundamental to individuals and for corporate existence of persons, yet these rights need to be curtailed for the benefit of the generality of the people. In essence, the constitution re-emphasises the fact that no right is without bounds. Therefore, on account of defence, public safety, public order, public morality, or for the purpose of protecting the rights and freedom of other persons the rights hereinbefore mentioned would be curtailed.

This section however goes on to provide in its sub-section (3) that:

> An Act of the National Assembly shall not be invalidated by reason only that it provides for the taking, during periods of emergency, of measures that derogate from the provisions of section 30 or 32 of this constitution; but no such measures shall be taken in pursuance of any such act during any period of emergency save to the extent that those measures are reasonably justifiable for the purpose of dealing with the situation that exists during that period of emergency: Provided that nothing in this section shall authorise any derogation from the provisions of section 30 of this constitution, except in respect of death resulting from acts of war or authorise any derogation from the provisions of section 33(8) of this constitution.

The following phrases need be noted: (1) that sections 30 and 32 shall not be derogated from even during a period of emergency. The purport of this provision is that some measures need be taken during a period of emergency for the purpose of protecting the whole public or the corporate existence of a nation. Where this occurs the interest of an individual must step down for the interest of the nation or the public. The measures taken in this regard must however be reasonably justifiable. The idea of justification in this regard is akin to what had earlier been considered. Despite the seemingly wide powers granted to revoke individual rights during a period of emergency, it must be pointed out that the use of emergency power cannot be something to be determined from the strange world. It means that during this period, it still behoves the court to consider whether the exercise of emergency power in the circumstance is justifiable. Section 265 of the constitution states that a state of emergency can be taken to have arisen when the nation is

(a) at war

(b) is in imminent danger of invasion or involvement in a state of war

(c) there is actual breakdown of public order and public safety in the federation or any part thereof to such extent as to require extraordinary measures to restore peace and security;

(d) there is a clear and present danger of an individual breakdown of public order and public safety in the federation or any part thereof requiring extraordinary measures to avert the same.

(e) there is an occurrence of imminent danger, or the occurrence of any disaster or national calamity, affecting the community or section of the community in the Federation;

(f) there is any other public danger which clearly constitutes a threat to the existence of the Federation; or

(g) a request is received to do so.

From the above instances, the determination of whether or not a state of emergence exists is necessarily a question of fact. In case of any dispute or if any question arises in respect of a declaration of a state of emergency and the assertion of any of the fundamental rights by a citizen, it should be possible for a court to determine whether in truth and in fact, the state of affairs is such that calls for the application of the emergency power provisions granted by the constitution.

Guidance in this respect could be sought from decided cases. In *Liversidge* v *Anderson*[14] by reason of World War II in Britain, the Emergency Power (Defence) Act 1939 gave Her Majesty, the power to make by Order in Council Regulations which appeared to him to be necessary or expedient for the public safety, defence of the realm and maintenance of public order. Following this, several Regulations were made. For example, Regulation 18B of the Defence (General) Regulations 1939 was made which provided that the Secretary of State on reasonable cause shown that any person was of hostile origin or association may make an order against that person directing for his detention. In consequence of this, the Secretary of State for Home Affairs acting in good faith issued an Order of detention under the order. The House of Lords was faced with the consideration of the scope and meaning of the Regulation as it affected personal liberty. The court held that the determination of whether it was reasonable in the circumstance to detain Liversidge was a subjective one and not an impersonal standard independent of the mind of the Secretary of State.

In Nigeria, following the fracas on the floor of the Western House of Assembly, the Federal Government declared a state of emergency. The Federal Government thus took over the administration of Western State. In the case of *Williams* v *Majekodunmi*[15] which ensued, Ademola C.J.F. held that in respect of issues dealing with the validity of the Emergency Powers Act 1961, the existence or non-existence of a state of

---

[14] (1942) A.C. 206.
[15] (1962) 1 All NLR 413.

public emergency was a "matter apparently within the bounds of Parliament, and not for this court to decide." It was also maintained that this position cannot change even if the declaration of the state of emergency by Parliament was made for political reasons.

Furthermore, in *Adegbenro* v *Attorney General of the Federation & 4 Ors*,[16] the court held:

> it is unnecessary for us to rule on the submission that parliament acted *mala fide* in making a declaration of a state of public emergency…since it is impossible to say in the present case that there was no ground to justify a declaration.[17]

Aihe and Oluyede[18] are of the view that it is not the duty of any court, according to the provision of section 70 of the 1963 constitution, to decide when there is a state of public emergency, but that of Parliament.

Having regard to the provision of section 265 of the 1979 Constitution and the combined effect of section 41(2) of the 1979 Constitution, it is doubtful if the same conclusion can be reached in relation to the power of the court to inquire into the validity or otherwise of the declaration of a state of emergency. Akande[19] commenting on the provisions of the law under the 1979 Constitution maintains that "these provisions would seem to have conferred upon the executive the power to declare periods of emergency but the discretion to determine what laws

---

[16] (1962) WNLR 150 at 160.

[17] See Aihe & Oluyede, *Cases and Materials on Constitutional Law in Nigeria*, Oxford University Press (1979) pp 73 – 75.

[18] Akande, *Introduction to the Nigerian Constitution*, Sweet & Maxwell, commentary on section 41 of the Constitution

[19] Further comments on section 41 of the constitution.

are reasonably justifiable in a democratic society is left with the legislature and the constitutionality of such law is excluded from judicial review." She however maintains that "the door is open under these provisions for judicial review of actions taken under such laws." The distinction drawn between the first view and the second is without a difference. A better view, it is submitted, is that while the bodies granted the power to declare a state of emergency may do so, the courts are not precluded from inquiring into the validity or otherwise of such declaration more so when the validity or otherwise of such declaration may be at stake.

Notwithstanding the ambiguity inherent in the provision that "the enactments of the National Assembly shall not be invalidated" by reason only that it provides for measures that derogate from rights to life and personal liberty, the courts, under section 6(6)(c) have the right to inquire into the validity or otherwise of the exercise of the power. The court should not abdicate its power or function to do justice. As the court rightly pointed out in *Adegbenro* v *Attorney-General of the Federation*:[20]

> These words…must be read in the context of the constitution and more particularly in the context of Chapter III in which they occur. The chapter confers certain fundamental rights which are regarded as essential and which are to be maintained and preserved; and they are to serve as a norm or legislation under majority rule, which is the form of rule pervading the constitutions. If they are to be invaded at all it must be only to the extent that it is essential for the sake of recognized public interest and may not be farther.

---

[20] (1962) WNLR, 150

To say the above is not to close one's eyes to the special period of emergency. The position however is that where there is truly a period of emergency, it would be patent that the curtailment of a person's fundamental right is for public good, order, safety or defence. But to make this a rule which validates the *mala fide* use of executive or legislative power is to kill the spirit of the constitution.

It is necessary to mention a particular Decree that tried to curtail freedom of the press. The Decree was titled 'The public Officers (Protection Against false Accusation) Decree No 4 of 1984. It protected public officers from public discussion of matters concerning them, no matter the truth of the issue. The decree was ultimately repealed in 1985.

There is nothing as good as a virile environment that ensures freedom of speech and the press. Freedom of speech and the press should not be done away with in order to ensure the dawn of a virile nation.

2

Disclosure of source of information

A necessary follow-up to freedom of expression and the press is the believe that the constitution guarantees free flow of information dissemination, education and entertainment. It is a known fact that a person who is defamed can sue for defamation. The same goes for a person who has brought the administration of justice to disrepute or ridicule. A person can also be charged with sedition in appropriate cases. The issue which needs be pointed out is, may a journalist or editor or a person charged to court on account of a particular publication maintain, on being asked to disclose his source of information that he cannot be compelled to disclose the source of his information? This issue will be examined against the background of decided cases and constitutional provisions.

Section 36 of the 1979 Constitution provides:

(1) Every person shall be entitled to freedom of expression, including freedom to hold opinions and to receive and impart ideas and information without interference.
(2) Without prejudice to the generality of subsection (1) of this section, every person shall be entitled to own, establish and operate any medium for the dissemination of information, ideas and opinions:

Provided that no person, other than the Government of the Federation or of a state or any other person or body authorised by the president, shall own, establish or operate a television or wireless broadcasting station for any purpose whatsoever.

(3) Nothing in this section shall invalidate any law that is reasonably justifiable in a democratic society

(a) for the purpose of preventing the disclosure of information received in confidence, maintaining the authority and independence of courts or regulating telephone, wireless broadcasting, television or the exhibition of cinematograph films: or

(b) imposing restrictions upon persons holding office under the Government of the Federation or of a state, members of the armed forces of the Federation or members of the Nigeria Police Force."

Given this provision of the law it is felt that the interest of the public is best served if free information dissemination is allowed, if public officials are not unnecessarily shielded as to make their activities not subject to public scrutiny and if citizens would be encouraged to give vital information on issues of public interest. In *British Steel Corporation* v *Granada Television Ltd.,*[1]

Lord Denning held as follows:

The public has a right of access to information which is of public concern and of which the public ought to know. The newspapers are the agents, so to speak, of the public to collect that information and to tell the public of it. In support of this right of access, the newspapers should not in general be compelled to disclose their sources of information. Neither by means of discovery before trial. Nor by questions or cross-examination at the trial. Nor by subpoena. The reason is because, if they were compelled to disclose their sources, they would soon be bereft of information which

[1] (1981) I All ER 417 at 441

they ought to have. Their sources would dry up. Wrongdoing would not be disclosed. Charlatans would not be exposed. Unfairness would go unremedied. Misdeeds in the corridors of power, in companies or in government departments would never be known. Investigative journalism has proved itself as a valuable adjunct of the freedom of the press.

It is in this regard that section 36 of the Constitution among other sections is hallowed. But beyond this measure of constitutionally permissive assertion, it should not be forgotten that section 41 of the constitution curtails the operation of section 36 in the following language:

Nothing in sections 34, 35, 36, 37 and 38 of this Constitution shall invalidate any law that is reasonably justifiable in a democratic society -
(a) in the interest of defence, public safety, public order, public morality or public health, or
(b)   for the purpose of protecting the rights and freedom of other persons.

The question that one needs to ask is whether by this provision, the operation of section 36 of the Constitution is rendered nugatory.

Before a detailed analysis of these provisions is embarked upon, it is necessary to have a look at what obtains in other jurisdictions.

In *Kilbourn* v *Thompson*,[2] the Supreme Court of the United States held thus:

---

[2] 103 U.S. 168p. 377

> The Committee...had no lawful authority to require Kilbourn to testify as a witness beyond what he voluntarily chose to tell, and the orders and resolutions of the house and the warrant of the speaker under which Kilbourn was imprisoned for refusal to testify before such committee, are void for want of jurisdiction in that body...[3]

The court in this case emphasised the authority of the American Constitution as the reference point in the determination of the authority of the court or any person and in particular in respect of duty alloting measures.

In the English case of *British Steel Corporation* v *Granada Television Ltd.*,[4] in January 1980, during a national steel strike by British Steel Corporation (B.S.C.) employees, a television company (Granada) decided to broadcast a programme on the strike. A few days before the programme Granada received copies of 250 secret and confidential documents from BSC's files relating to internal actions and discussions at a high level within BSC and between BSC and the government. The documents were received unsolicited from an unofficial source, who was clearly someone inside BSC who had access to them, and showed possible mismanagement within BSC. Granada used 27 of them in their programme. The informant was not revealed in accordance with a promise by Granada to him that his identity would not be disclosed. BSC brought proceedings against Granada seeking, *inter alia*, an order that Granada disclose the identity of the informant. BSC contended that it was necessary for them to know the identity of the informant in order to prevent further misuse of BSC documents, possibly by an injunction, and to remove the suspicion directed at those of their

---

[3] At p. 378
[4] (1981) I All E.R. 417

staff who had access to the documents. On the hearing of the motion, the judge ordered Granada to disclose the identity of the informant, and that order was upheld by the Court of Appeal. Granada appealed to the House of Lords, contending (I) that BSC was not entitled to obtain the name of the informant by what was in substance an action for discovery because, *inter alia*, newspapers and broadcasting authorities were in a special position regarding being compelled to disclose information, as was illustrated by the 'newspaper rule' which protected newspapers from the requirement that a defendant in a libel action should disclose the source of his information on discovery, (ii) that disclosure could not be ordered against Granada because it was not required to assist either existing or intended proceedings against the informant, there being no evidence that BSC would bring an action against him, (iii) that disclosure of the identity of the informant by Granada would tend to incriminate them and (iv) that the court ought to exercise its discretion by refusing to order such disclosure because of the public interest that the public should be informed about the steel strike and BSC's conduct of their affairs. The court, on account of the above, held as follows:

(i) Although the courts had an inherent wish to respect the confidentiality of information obtained as the result of a particular relationship, including the relationship between a journalist and his sources, journalists and the information media had no immunity based on public interest protecting them from the obligation to disclose their sources of information in court if such disclosure was necessary in the interests of justice. The 'newspaper rule' was confined to libel actions and did not extend to actions based on breach of confidence and hence did not operate to confer on newspapers and broadcasting authorities a general immunity from disclosure of their sources.

(ii) BSC were *prima facie* entitled to an order that Granada disclose the identity of their informant because (a) in becoming involved in their informant's tortious act in removing the documents from BSC without authority, Granada would have been under a duty to assist BSC by disclosing the identity of the wrongdoer even if they had been involved through no fault of their own, and *a fortiori* they were under a duty having used the documents for their own purposes while knowing their removal to have been unauthorised (b) BSC were not seeking discovery for the mere gratification of curiosity but had suffered a wrong for which they had a real and unsatisfied claim against the informant and could not bring any proceedings against him until Granada revealed his identity. The conditions for granting the remedy sought therefore existed.

(iii) Granada were not able to rely on the defence that disclosure of the informant's identity might tend to incriminate them because even if there was a real and appreciable risk of Granada being prosecuted for the offences of handling stolen goods and conspiracy to defraud by infringing BSC's copyright in the documents, the disclosure of the informant's identity would not strengthen the case against Granada since Granada had already stated in evidence all the matters which might disclose an offence and the disclosure of a name by Granada incriminating itself by its own evidence. Neither could Granada claim privilege under the 'iniquity rule' because the documents had not revealed any iniquity or misconduct by BSC.

(iv) If BSC were to be confined to their remedy against Granada and denied the opportunity of a remedy against the informant there would be a significant denial of justice, and the strong public interest in doing justice outweighed any public interest that the public should be informed about the steel strike. The balance of the court's discretion whether to order disclosure of the source came down strongly in BSC's favour.

The conclusion of the court in asking for disclosure in this case could be said to be based on the reasoning put forward by the court in *Attorney-General* v *Mulholland* by Lord Denning to the effect that:

A judge is the person entrusted, on behalf of the community, to weigh these conflict of interests - to weigh on the one hand the respect due to confidence in the profession and on the other hand the ultimate interest of the community in justice being done...If the judge determines that the journalist must answer, then no privilege will avail him to refuse.

In order to protect the press, in England, section 10 of the Contempt of Court Act 1981 was enacted. It provides:

No court may require a person to disclose... the source of information contained in a publication for which he is responsible, unless it be established to the satisfaction of the court that disclosure is necessary in the interests of justice or national security or for the prevention of disorder or crime.

The operation of this Act came up for consideration in *Secretary of State for Defence & Anor* v *Guardian Newspapers Ltd.*[6] A document classified "secret" was prepared in the Ministry of Defence. Seven copies of the document were sent from the Ministry to the Prime Minister, senior Ministers, the

---

[5] (1963) I All E.R. 767 at 771

[6] (1985) A.C. 339

Chief whip and the Secretary of the Cabinet. A photocopy of the document was delivered to the defendant newspaper. The editor, who did not know how or by whom the document had been delivered, concluded after inquiries that it was authentic and published its contents. On the Secretary of State's request for the immediate return of the document, which bore certain markings which was believed could aid the identification of the informant, the defendants claimed that by virtue of section 10 of the contempt of Court Act 1981 they could not be required to disclose the source of their information and said that they would only return the document with the markings excised.

By writ and notice of motion the Crown claimed that the copyright in infringing copies of the secret document was vested in the Crown and sought an order for the immediate delivery of the document in the defendant's possession. Scott J. held that section 10 of the Contempt of Court Act 1981 was not intended to interfere with proprietary rights and that the Crown was entitled to the order sought. The majority of the Court of Appeal expressed doubts as to the application of section 10 to proprietary claims but all held that on an assumption that it did so apply the interest of "justice" and "national security" required the immediate return of the document and accordingly those exceptions to the operation of section 10 of the Act of 1981 regarding the immunity from disclosure of a source of information had been established and an order for the delivery of the document was made. On appeal, the House of Lords held that on its true construction, section 10 of the contempt of Court Act 1981 applied to all judicial proceedings irrespective of their nature, or the claim or cause of action in respect of which they had been brought. The court further held that although the defendants were *prima facie* entitled to the protection of the section it was however removed by the crown adducing evidence sufficient to discharge the onus of showing that immediate delivery of the document was necessary in the interests of national security.

In *Re An Inquiry Under the Company Securities (Insider dealing) Act 1985*,[7] the business correspondent of a national newspaper published two articles in which he accurately forecast the result of inquiries made by the Monopolies and Mergers Commission and the Office of Fair Trading into two take-over bids. It was apparent from the articles that in writing them the journalist had used information leaked to him from an official source or given to him by a source close to the leak. Inspectors appointed by the Secretary of State to investigate suspected leaks from government departments of price-sensitive information about take-over bids requested the journalist pursuant to section 177 (3) of the Financial Services Act 1986, to reveal the sources of his information on which the articles were based. The journalist refused to divulge his sources and the inspectors certified the matter under section 178 of the 1986 Act for an inquiry by the Court into his refusal. Under section 178 (2) (a) the court could, if it was satisfied that the refusal was made without reasonable excuse, punish it as if it were a contempt of court. The judge dismissed the inspector's application on the ground that the journalist had a 'reasonable excuse' within section 178 (2) for refusing to comply with the inspector's request. On appeal by the inspectors, the Court of Appeal held that, as was the case under section 10 of the Contempt of Court Act 1981, what would otherwise be a reasonable excuse would not avail the journalist if it was established that disclosure of its sources was "necessary...for the prevention of...crime." The court further held that the inspectors had established that disclosure of its source was "necessary...for

---

[7] (1988) I E.R. 203

the prevention of...crime." The journalist appealed to the House of Lords, contending that the inspectors had not identified the particular crime which was sought to be prevented. The House of Lords held that on the true construction of section 10 of the 1981 Act a person could be in contempt for refusing to disclose his sources of information if the disclosure was necessary for the prevention of crime generally rather than a particular identifiable future crime. Accordingly, the court held, since the purpose of the inspector's inquiry was to expose the leaking of official information and criminal insider trading and to consider measures to prevent future leaks and insider trading and since, on the evidence, the journalist's information was necessary for that purpose, the journalist could not avail himself of the protection of section 10 but was required to reveal his sources on pain of being committed for contempt under section 178 (2) of the 1986 Act. The appeal was consequently dismissed.

In construing Article 10 of the Contempt of Court Act, Lord Templeman in *A.G.* v *Guardian Newspapers Ltd.*[8] relied on the judgment of the European Court to the effect that:

> (The European Court) is faced not with a choice between two conflicting principles but with a principle of freedom of expression that is narrowly interpreted...It is not sufficient that the interference involved belongs to that class of exceptions listed in Article 10 which has been invoked; neither is it sufficient that the interference was imposed because its subject-matter fell within a particular category or was caught by a rule formulated in general or absolute terms: the Court has to be satisfied that the interference was necessary having regard to the facts and circumstances prevailing in the specific case before it.

---

[8] (1987) 3 All E.R. 316 at 355 - 356.

It is now necessary to consider the position in Nigeria. In *Tony Momoh* v *Senate of the National Assembly & Ors*,[9] Tony Momoh, the editor of the *Daily Times* newspaper was summoned by the Senate to give the details of a publication in the 'GRAPEVINE' column of the *Daily Times* of 4th February, 1980 about Senators and their act in lobbying for contracts from the executive arm of government. The editor challenged the summons on the ground that it was a violation of his right to freedom of expression guaranteed by the Constitution. The court in delivering its judgment recognised the purport of section 36(1) as that which guarantees freedom to hold opinions and to receive and impart ideas and information. Section 36(2) was also taken to include newspaper publication in this context. In construing the application of section 36 of the 1979 Constitution to the issue before it, Ademola Johnson Ag. C.J. held:

> It is a matter of common knowledge that those who express their opinions, or impart ideas and information through the medium of a newspaper or any other medium for the dissemination of information enjoy by customary law and convention a degree of confidentiality. How else is a dissemination of information to operate if those who supply him with such information are not assured of protection from identification and/or disclosure.[10]

The court concluded thus:

> Without straining words it appears clear that any attempt to force a person as the applicant who disseminates information through the medium of a newspaper to disclose the source of information apparently given in confidence is

---

[9] (1981) I NCLR 105
[10] At pg. 113

an interference with 'the freedom of expression without interference' granted by section 36(1).

The court cautioned on the temptation of relying on foreign decisions on this issue. In the words of the court:

> The views expressed by the learned CJ is typical of that applicable in a Parliamentary system of government. Ours is a presidential system of government with a written Constitution. In Parliamentary system practised by the courts in England to which the learned CJ made special reference and cited cases decided under that system, it must be noted that a material distinguishing factor between the two systems is that the English Constitution is unwritten and made up of customs, tradition and conventions. Ours is written, its provisions are supreme and each arm of government is restricted to the powers conferred under the said written constitution.[11]

It should be pointed out that the court did not consider the implication of section 41 vis-à-vis section 36 of the 1979 Constitution in the case of *Tony Momoh* v *The Senate of the National Assembly*.[12] This issue, among others, was considered in *Innocent Adikwu (Editor, Sunday Punch Newspapers) & Ors.* v *Federal House of Representatives of the National Assembly & Ors.*[13] The applicants were journalists - The first applicant was an editor of the *Sunday Punch*. They received letters of invitation from the Committee of the House of Representatives of the National Assembly to appear at diverse dates to testify on the information contained in the publication of *Sunday Punch* titled 'Fraud - Legislators claim Salaries and Allowances for

---

[11] At pg. 114
[12] *Supra*
[13] (1982) 3 NCLR 394

fictitious staff' of 5th April, 1981. They applied under the Fundamental Rights (Enforcement Procedure) Rules 1979 to enforce their Fundamental Rights complaining that the action of the House of Representatives amounted to an interference with their constitutional rights under section 36 of the 1979 Constitution and enforceable under section 42 of the said Constitution. Balogun A.L.A.L.J., held *inter alia*:[14]

> It must be remembered at all times that a free press is one of the pillars of freedom in this country as indeed in any democratic society. A free press reports matters of general public importance, and cannot, in law be under an obligation, save in exceptional circumstances to disclose the identity of the persons who supply it with the information appearing in its report. Section 36 of the constitution which guarantees freedom of speech and expression (and press freedom) does provide a constitutional protection of free flow of information. In respect of the press, the editor's or reporter's constitutional right to a confidential relationship with his source stems from that constitutional guarantee. It is the basic concern that underlies the constitutional guarantee of freedom of speech and expression. If this right does not exist or is not protected by the courts when contravened or when there is a likelihood of its being contravened, the press's sources of information would dry up and the public would be deprived of being informed of many matters of great public importance. This must not be allowed to happen in a free and democratic society. In a country with a written Constitution which establishes a constitutional structure involving a tripartite allocation of power to the legislation, the executive and the Judiciary as coordinate organs of government, the judiciary as the guardian of the fundamental law of the land has the role of passing on the

---

[14] At p. 417

validity of the exercise of powers by the Legislative and Executive and to require them to observe the Constitution of the land.

In relation to the extent of recognition of freedom of expression and the press guaranteed by section 36 of the 1979 Constitution, the court held that this section is subject to the "built in limitations and exceptions to that section which restricts fundamental right of freedom of speech, ideas and expression."[15]

The court then concluded:

> In my view it seems clear that the circumstances of this case are neither grave nor exceptional, and therefore do not fall within the permissible limitations of freedoms provided for under chapter IV of the Constitution in the built in exceptions or limitations or otherwise.

It could therefore be concluded that the constitution recognises freedom of expression and the press. No one can take away these rights except as recognised by the built-in provisions in Chapter IV of the said Constitution. To say this however, is not to close one's eyes to the reality of the position under the Military. This is because the constitutional provision relating to freedom of expression and the press may be curtailed or indeed taken away by a decree. For example, a person may be imprisoned for non-disclosure of his source of information under Decree 2 or as it happened in respect of Decree 4 of 1984 when it was in existence.

---

[15] This is section 41 of the 1979 Constitution.

It is beyond doubt that freedom of expression and the press should not be toyed with. In a democratic setting one can be sure or assured of the recognition of freedom of expression and the press and the protection of the editor or the good spirited individual who decides to give the public the benefit of knowing what is happening in government or in respect of an issue of public importance, relevance and interest. Except this is done, the press's sources of information will dry up and the editor's or reporter's constitutional right to a confidential relationship with his source of information will be a mirage. Much as the constitutional provision relating to freedom of expression and the press is hallowed, one must not forget to note the cautionary words of Denning M. R. In *British Steel Corporation* v *Granada Television Ltd.*[16] that:

> in order to be deserving of freedom, the press must show itself worthy of it. A free press must be a responsible press. The power of the press is great. It must not abuse its power. If a newspaper should act irresponsibly, then it forfeits its claim to protect its sources of information." In relation to Nigeria therefore, it could be asserted that the law recognises the right of the journalist to protect or refuse to disclose his source of information except as curtailed by relevant provisions of the law dealing with defence, public safety, public order, public morality or public health or for the purpose of protecting the rights and freedom of other persons.

---

[16] *Supra* at pg. 441.

3

Writing techniques

The primary work of a journalist is communication of ideas or issues to others. The knowledge or wisdom of any person is of value only if it can be communicated. It is often said that he who knows but cannot express what he knows might as well be ignorant or in its Latin expression *qui novit neque id quod sentit exprimit perinde ext ac si nesciret.*[1]

The beauty of any communication therefore depends on the effort of the reader or speaker to communicate effectively. Communication is like the arrow that hits the target. As Fowler[2] pointed out:

> Anyone who wishes to become a good writer should endeavour, before he allows himself to be tempted by the more showy qualities to be direct, simple, brief, vigorous and lucid.

Except a journalist is careful, he may end up in jail as his speech or script may contain scandalous, defamatory or seditious content. It therefore behoves every journalist to be sure of what he writes. It is necessary to emphasise the legal aspect

---

[1] Weinhofen H., Legal Writing Style, St. Paul Minn. West Publishing Co. 1980 p.1.
[2] H.W. & F.G. Fowler, *The King's English*.

of written communication. In *Engineering Enterprise* v *A.G. Kaduna*,[3] Oputa JSC held that the ABC of all legal writing are accuracy, brevity and clarity. It is however necessary to add a fourth requirement which is order.

Accuracy

This requires ability to present an issue in a honest and straightforward manner. Since facts are sacred, what is being put across must be factual and to the point. The factual situation must not be confused by the use of unnecessary style. According to White:[4]

> Style is not a garnishment for the meat of prose, a sauce by which a dull fish is made palatable. Style has no such separate entity; it is non-detachable, unfilterable. The beginner should approach style warily, realising that it is himself he is approaching, no other.

The reader of a document should be able to determine the precise intention of the writer. A mistake in this regard may spoil a good case. A writer's writings distil all his research.

It must however be acknowledged that many of the English words are ambiguous. A writer must however strive to control them. Occasionally, the subject-matter a writer is dealing with may be very complex such that except he is very careful, his writing may be weakened by equivocating words like 'generally' or 'as a general rule'. Caution and reticence in writing, noted Justice Frankfurter, "make for qualifications and

---

[3] (1987) 2 NWLR (pt. 57) 413.
[4] White E.B., *The Elements of Style with Revisions: An Introduction and a New Chapter on Writing* (1959). P.18.

circumlocutions that stifle spontaneity, slow the rhythm of speech, check the play of imagination...[5]

Mr. Justice Holmes has rightly pointed out that "to philosophise" in this regard, "is to generalise but to generalise is to omit". A journalist is expected to exercise judgment and a sense of what is material and what can be omitted. Making sweeping statements without giving attention to their relevance may have fatal consequences. The following must therefore be noted:

(i)   When an exact word cannot be found, take time to find it or consult a dictionary.

(ii) When in doubt of a word, look it up.

(iii) When an appropriate word cannot be found, consider re-writing the clause or sentence another way.

Brevity

It is fallacious to think that one's writing will be appreciated if it could be laid out in a number of pages. This conclusion may result in the writing becoming unnecessarily lengthy, verbose, clumsy and meaningless.

Economy of language is a good strategy in writing. If a man can be convinced by 20 pages of precise and relevant write-up, he cannot be more convinced by 100. In fact, 100 pages of verbose and irrelevant write-up may bore the reader. He may even change his mind altogether by reason of fatigue, resentment, forgetfulness or lack of lustre.

Be brief not only in the whole, but in the parts. Each sentence should be brief, direct and free of words that fail to advance the meaning of the issue you wish to put across. It must offer more thought than words, characterise rather than catalogue, accent

[5] Weinhofen *Op cit.* p.11

the idea instead of the detail, strike a profile instead of photographing; indeed, to be able, it is sufficient to "proceed allusively". By this progression brevity merges into brilliance. The above does credit to the writer, a contrary approach paints the writer dull and uninspiring.

Order

A writer must be orderly in his presentation. The writer's art is more like that of the motion picture director, who must present one film after another in rapid succession. The audience or reader must be able to follow the writer. As one writer puts it: "word must follow word in an orderly procession; and when the last word has filed into its place, the whole army should be found drawn up so as to present exactly the formation from which it started." Suppose a regiment massed in the form of a square, is ordered to pass through an opening too narrow to admit more than one man at a time, and to form upon the other side in the same square formation. As the men pass from one place through the opening into another, so the words must pass from your mind by ear or eye into the mind of another; and as the men break off from the square, rank by rank, in a certain order, and fall in again in the same order, so must the words progress from your mind and rearrange themselves in a certain order. Then, when the process is complete, they will be found drawn up in the mind of another, in the same formation as that in which they are drawn up in your own mind.[6]

An orderly writing is always beautiful to behold. In order to have an orderly writing, the following precepts may be observed,

---

[6] Quoted in Robbing, *An Approach to Composition Through Psychology* pp. 84 - 85.

(i) An outline of the goal of the writer should be made. An outline will help the writer achieve the following goals -
   (a) the entire ground will be covered;
   (b) the writing will develop logically from the first step to the last; and
   (c) the writing will take a balanced and coherent shape. The function of an outline to a piece of writing, is like that of the human skeleton to the body. It gives it shape.

(ii) The reader should be able to know constantly how the writing progresses. Each new step should follow the other before so naturally as to seem inevitable.

This would give the writing logical sequence. The work will naturally be interesting to read.

Titles and headings emphasise the organisation and lead the reader by hand, especially the hasty reader who has no time to read the whole essay. He may wish to take in a page at a glance. If the landscape is clear, perhaps he can. This can be achieved if appropriate titles and headings are made use of. In relation to the headings and sub-headings, the essential concepts should be identified and they should be expressed in a flash. A new one must be used the moment there is a change of thought. Numbers and letters emphasise their relationship.

The reader should be able to know what is being said or where the writer is going.

Each sentence must fit into the overall plan. Essential issues should be emphasised. If secondary matters must be mentioned, do so in a footnote or a following sentence. If you have two thoughts use two sentences. Never put 2 in 1, for one may kick the other out of bed or indeed each may do so, leaving a meaningless message.

Clarity

Clarity is the keystone of good writing.[7] Good sentences and short English words are simple to understand than long ones. They give punch to writing. As Sloane stated:

> Frequent short paragraphs with introducing captions are easier to follow than pages of solidly set type. Remember that the more difficult the problem the shorter the reader's attention span. Don't coddle him with primers. But don't confuse him with intricate metaphors and a display of verbal fireworks either.

As one writer puts it, he who speaks in parables may need a commentator, but may not get one. In order to determine whether a particular writing is clear, these two questions may be asked:

      (i)   Do you, the writer understand it?
      (ii)   Will the reader understand it?

The issue is not whether the reader understands it per se but whether he understands it in the same way that the writer is putting it across.

The reader should not be made to struggle or turn back to get the meaning of what is being put across. He may skip instead and think about his own problems. He may come to the conclusion that if your words are dubious, your case is weak.

Gibson[8] has suggested the following as aids to clear writing:

---

[7] Morris L. Cohen, *How to Find the Law*, Chapter 18, West Publishing Co., P.18, 466.

[8] Gibson G.D., *Elements of Style*, p. 547.

(a) Use simple homespun words, preferably of Anglo-Saxon origin and the shorter the better.

(b) Use verbs and nouns thus minimising adjectives and adverbs.
The former are the meat, the latter the sauce.

(c) Be specific. Avoid the diffuse and hesitate before venturing on "full generalisation".

(d) Be wary of metaphors, for they may have disturbing implications.

(e) Alert the reader to the nature of what is to come by a sensitive use of 'and', 'but', 'though' and such connective phrases.

(f) Use the same word always for the same idea. Elegant variations are confusing and in poor taste.

(g) Avoid obscure or technical phrases as far as possible and avoid Latin always.

(h) Avoid unfamiliar references. An executive will not be pleased to be told that something is as scarce as "owls in Iceland" since only an ornithologist knows that none is there. You should note that a wounded reader is a resentful one.

(i) Accept as a premise that a legalism is a solecism.

(j) Avoid repetitions and duplications. An arrow has a single shaft.

(k) Avoid unnecessary detail, or your arrow will never fly.

(l) Avoid decoration until you are a master, it will at best confuse, at worst repel. Adjectives and eloquence may be saved for home use or amateur theatricals. When you are a master, you will make your own rules.

Some of the above hints overlap but they combine to state the framework of a good writing. A single hour spent on pruning

and sharpening a written work will do more for its clarity than
many hours of amplifying and explaining. An obscure writing
does nobody any good. Suppose that a student is preparing for
his first tutorial in Jurisprudence (Science of Law). He sits in the
Library with an article from his reading list open in front of him.
He reads as follows:

> The predictive empiricism inherent in the neo-thomist
> rejection of metaphysics qua metaphysics typically
> characterises the substance epistemology so clearly
> demonstrated by Weberstrom's implicit acceptance of the
> semantically normative assertions made by Haranmere in all
> his later work on voluntarist teleology. But the question
> arises as to why it was that Haranmere's conceptualisation
> of platonic ontology placed him so firmly in the ranks of
> those who believed the cognitism in its contractarian form is
> no support for Weberstrom's analysis of the Kelsenian
> grundnorm. This is the question that must be faced.

The answer which such a student would give is that such a
question must indeed be faced. He would not have understood a
word he has read.

Apart from the basic points stated above, it should be noted
that some pitfalls to good writing are recognised.[9] It is therefore
necessary to note these basic factors that may inhibit good
writing. They include:

(1) Opening statement:

The opening statement introduces the topic or issue in focus.
This must arouse the interest of the reader. This interest must be
sustained so that the whole of the essay may be read. An

---

[9] See Sloane R., *Legal Writing*, Chapter 18, West Publishing Co., Pp. 467 - 469.

opening statement that promotes little understanding and no desire to continue reading stands in the same position as an introductory statement taken from a foreign language not understood by the reader.

George Bernard Shaw once wrote that a playwright should tell his audience what he is going to say; then he should say it; and finally he should tell them he has said it.

Obscurity

An old adage says there is nothing so simple that the mind of man cannot complicate. An obscure writing hides the true intent of the writer and this does no credit to him. An obscure writing may not be worth the paper on which such is written. An obscure writing may be caused by any of these faults:

     (i)   muddling
     (ii)   overblowing; or
     (iii)   pomposity.

Such writings have the effect of producing more razzledazzle than reason, dignity but not wit. For example, it would simply have been enough to say "academic sycophants" instead of saying in too much a clumsy expression:

"There are in the ivory towers some ready versatility of convictions and a staunch devotion to their bread."

Vogue words

A vogue word is that which has been used and used again i.e. one made trite by over-use. A writer should not form the habit of using vogue words. Reliance on vogue words has the effect of branding the writer a copycat instead of an originator.

Furthermore, while a creative writer is a sculptor, the copycat is a mere embalmer. It is profitable to be distinct in one's style, that makes for creativity and originality. It should be borne in mind that the word that is now referred to as a vogue word was once used for the first time by another person.

Letters

A well written letter is a work of art. The four rules stated above i.e. brevity, clarity, order and accuracy must be obeyed. Before any letter is written, the question must first be asked, is this letter necessary? A telephone call, a meeting or even silence may be preferable.

A letter must be properly addressed. If a letter is mis-addressed, it may be delayed or lost. If there is any error in the spelling of the name of the addressee, he may resent the letter rather than appreciate it.

A short descriptive caption across the top of a letter alerts the reader to its subject and assists both the writer and reader in filing it and later recalling it from a file if and when it is needed.[10] The writer should indicate the issue he is discussing by a short title across the middle of the page. If a short title is conspicuously placed, the word "Re" may be unnecessary. It is not elegant to refer below "to the above caption, case or matter". It could be assumed that the reader would appreciate that you will not designate one subject and then discuss another. In *Nimanters Association* v *Marco Construction Co. Ltd & Ors.*,[11] the Court of Appeal held that where there is a "conflict between the heading of a letter and its body, the latter prevails as the

---

[10] Cohen M.L. *Op cit.* pp. 469 - 476.
[11] (1991) 2 NWLR (pt. 174) 411.

heading of a letter is only a descriptive precis or paraphrase by the writer of the subject."

A wide margin at the left side of a letter permits securing it with fasteners in a file folder. Furthermore, additional space may draw the reader's attention to what has been written.

The writer's name should be typed below his signature. Otherwise a reply may be addressed to some non-existent person suggested by the illegible hierophyph set down as a signature.

Whatever may be the conclusion, a good letter must be clear and definite. The conclusion should be stated in a manner that is hand-tailored. It should be remembered that your letter is your representative. It speaks for you when you are absent. Though it cannot answer questions. The questions must therefore be anticipated.

Any letter is successful if it accomplishes three things:

     (i)   excites the reader's interest at the onset;

     (ii)   holds his interest to the end, and

     (iii)   moves him to action.

Documents

Documents are more formal than letters, since no one expects to read them for fun but hope to have a business deal succinctly covered in all its aspect. The suggestions made for brevity, accuracy, clarity and order are also useful here.

In relation to formal matters, it is well to eliminate recitals unless they really fill a need. If they do, put them in a statement of background and propose in the way you would explain the document to the recipient. Definitions are invaluable unless your document is unusually simple. Where definitions are made, they should be used precisely, not approximately.

If the document involves a wholly new problem, analyse it first in steps, remembering that chronological order is helpful to the ordinary mind. Having established the successive points, discuss them in the same order. In all, it should be stated that your documents should be clear and unequivocal.

4

Defamation

One particular tort or crime that may be committed by a journalist is defamation. Each person cherishes his reputation. Where therefore there is an infraction on the reputation of any person in consequence of a false publication, such a person may sue for defamation. The justification for the recognition of this tort therefore is this: the law in its wisdom insists that words which are capable of leaving a stain on the reputation of another should not in the absence of lawful excuse be uttered or published of and concerning a person. The Court of Appeal in *Nigerian Television Authority* v *Ebenezer Babatope*[1] defined a defamatory statement thus:

> a defamatory statement is a statement which is published of and concerning a person and calculated to lower him in the estimation of right thinking person or cause him to be shunned or avoided, to expose him to hatred, contempt or ridicule or to convey an imputation on him disparaging or injurious to him in his office, profession, calling, trade or business.

[1] (1996) 4 NWLR (pt 440) 75

This was also the view of the court in *Sketch Publishing Co. Ltd.* v *Ajagbemokeferi.*[2]

By the nature of the definition of defamation a point that readily comes to mind is the determination of whether or not the statement is defamatory. The mirror through which this is determined is that of a reasonable man. Who then is a reasonable man in this context? According to *Winfield* and *Jolowiz*,[3] the reasonable man in this context is not a person who is so lax or so cynical that he would think none the worse of a man whatever was imputed to him, and on the other hand those who are so censorious as to regard even trivial accusations (if they were true) as lowering another's reputation, or who are so hasty as to infer the worst meaning from any ambiguous statement. Anyone who comes within the bracket of those discussed above cannot be regarded as a reasonable man for this purpose. The focus of our law therefore is on the ordinary citizen, whose judgment is taken as standard. He is neither unusually suspicious nor unusually naïve. The ordinary man in this context was described by Okunola JCA in *African Newspaper of Nigeria Ltd.* v *Adamu Ciroma*[4] thus:

> the ordinary and natural meaning of the words are to be seen from the eyes of a reasonable man of ordinary intelligence guided by a general knowledge and not from the eyes of a person who is fettered by legal rules of construction or forced into an unreasonable interpretation.

It should also be noted that the determination of a reasonable man is not necessarily a matter of classification. This is because

---

[2] (1989) 1 NWLR (pt 100) 678. See also *Esika* v *Medolu*, *infra*; *Din* v *African Newspapers of (Nig.) Ltd.* (1990) 3NWLR (pt 139) 392.

[3] Winfield & Jolowiz on *Tort*, Sweet & Maxwell 1979 11th Ed. Pg. 275

[4] (1996) 1 NWLR (pt 423) 156.

words, which may be frowned upon by a detached segment of the society, may not be so considered by the right-thinking members of the society.[5]

It should be stated that defamation may be a tort, it may also be a crime. In relation to the criminal aspect, section 374 of the Criminal Code provides thus:

> for the purpose of this code, the publication of defamatory matter is:
>
> (1) in the absence of spoken words or audible sounds, the speaking of such words or the making of such sounds in the hearing of the person defamed or any other person;
> (2) in other cases, the exhibiting it in public, or causing it to be read or seen, or showing, or delivering it, or causing it to be shown or delivered, with intent that it may be read or seen by the person defamed or by any other person.

Punishment for this offence is provided in section 375 of the Criminal Code.

Defamation consists of slander and libel. A libel relates to a defamatory statement or representation in permanent or written form. If the complaint relates to spoken word or gestures, it is slander. The question may be asked, what is the position of the defamatory statement which is synchronised with the photographic reproduction? In *Youssoupoff* v *Metro Goldwyn-Mayer Pictures Ltd*,[6] the court held that the defamatory statement contained in a "talking cinematograph film" was a libel. In the words of the court:

---

[5] See *Egbuna* v *Amalgamated Press of Nigeria* [1967] 1 All NLR 25
[6] (1934) 50 TLR 581

There can be no doubt that so far as the photographic part of the exhibition is concerned, that is a permanent matter to be seen by the eye, and is the proper subject of an action for libel, if defamatory. I regard the speech which is synchronised with the photographic reproduction and forms part of one complex, common exhibition as an ancillary circumstance, part of the surrounding that which is to be seen.

Distinction between libel and slander

Defamation, as stated above, consists of slander and libel. Slander relates to defamation in a transient form. This could be conveyed by words or gestures. Hence it is said that libel is addressed to the eye whilst slander is addressed to the ear. Libel on the other hand, relates to defamatory utterances and imputations conveyed in a permanent form as in writing, signs, pictures, paintings, cartoons, statues or films.

Furthermore, it should be noted that whereas libel is actionable *per se*, that is without proof of special (or actual) damage, slander is not actionable *per se* except in certain cases.

As a general rule, damage must be proved but in certain cases, slander is actionable without any proof of damage. Such cases include imputation of crime, imputation of disease, imputation of unchastity or adultery, imputation of unfitness or incompetence. The basis for this was eloquently stated by Brown L.J. in *Ratcliffe* v *Evans*[7] thus:

> Every libel is of itself a wrong in regard to which the law implies general damages.... Akin to action for libel are those actions which are brought for oral slander, where such

---

[7] (1892) 2 Q.B. 524 at 529-530

slander consists of words actionable per se, and the mere use of which constitute the infringement of the plaintiff's right. The very speaking of such words apart from damage, constitutes a wrong and gives rise to a cause of action. The law in such a case presumes.... general damages.

(a) Imputation of crime: where a crime punishable by imprisonment is alleged, this is actionable especially where there is a direct imputation of it and not just a mere suspicion of it. In *Jackson* v *Adams*[8] the defendant said of the plaintiff, a churchwarden, "you stole the parish bellropes, you scamping rascal?" This was held not to be defamatory, as the plaintiff was not in a position to steal the ropes. The position of the law in this regard relates to the effect of the imputation on the reputation of the plaintiff and not on the imprisonment which would have been the consequence of a conviction.

(b) Imputation of disease: Where a contagious or infectious disease is imputed in such a way that is likely to prevent other people from associating with the plaintiff, this is actionable *per se*. The disease in this regard may be due to the visitation of God, accident or the indiscretion of the party therewith afflicted.

(c) Imputation of unchastity or adultery: The requirement of the law here is for example, provided in section 4 of the Defamation Law of Oyo State. It provides that words spoken and published, which impute unchastity to any woman or girl shall not require special damage to render them actionable.

(d) Imputation of unfitness or Incompetence: The law has in focus the imputation of unfitness, dishonesty or

---

[8] (1835) 2 Bing N.C. 402

incompetence in any office, profession, calling, trade or business held or carried on by the plaintiff at the time when the slander was published. In *Onojioghfia* v *Okitipai*.[9] The plaintiff was referred to as a rogue who ran away " with my money and he is still on the run" these words were held not actionable *per se* because "although those words impute dishonesty and are injurious to the plaintiff and could be particularly harmful to him in the way of his business, they do not....impute dishonesty to him in his capacity as a building contractor." This decision, based on the common Law, cannot stand since there are provisions of the law to the contrary. For example section 5 of the Defamation law of Oyo State provides:

in an action for slander in respect of words calculated to disparage the plaintiff in any office, profession, calling, trade or business held or carried on by him at the time of publication it shall not be necessary to allege or prove special damage whether or not the words are spoken of the plaintiff in the way of his office, profession, calling, trade or business.

Vulgar abuse

Mere vulgar abuse does not constitute actionable slander. Whether an utterance constitutes vulgar abuse or not depends on the circumstances of the case. Mere general vituperation uttered in cold blood, or brawled out at the height of a violent quarrel does not constitute slander. The speaker of the words must

---

[9] (1974) 4 ECSLR 465

however take the risk of his hearers construing them as defamatory and not simply abusive. In *Bakare* v *Ishola*,[10] there was a fight preceded by an altercation between the two parties. In the heat of anger, the defendant said in the presence of onlookers "*Ole ni o. Elewon, iwo ti o sese ti ewon de yi*" meaning "You are a thief, ex- convict, you who have just come out of prison." This was taken to be a mere vulgar abuse. Jibowu C.J. observed thus:

> it is a matter of common knowledge of which this court takes judicial notice, that people commonly abuse each other as a prelude to a fight and call each other "ole! elewon! (thief, ex- convict) which abuse no one takes seriously as they are words of heat and anger.

In *Ibeanu* v *Uba*,[11] the spoken words were "Josiah, Josiah, Ongi kpo ndi ori bia zulu ewum, bia malu uma najum", meaning "Josiah, Josiah, you brought the thieves with whom you stole my goat and you have now come to ask me." These words were taken not to be mere vulgar abuse.

Where the words are contained in a written, not spoken form, they would not be regarded as mere vulgar abuse since the defendant would have had time to reflect before writing.

Essentials of defamation

In *Sketch* v *Ajagbemokeferi*,[12] the supreme court held that in an action for defamation, the onus is on the plaintiff to prove:

---

[10] (1959) WNLR 106
[11] (1972) 2 ESCLR 194
[12] (1989) 1 NWLR (Pt 100) 683.

(a) that the defendant published a statement and in the case of libel in a permanent form.

(b) that the statement referred to the plaintiff.

(c) that the statement conveys a defamatory meaning to those to whom it was published; and

(d) that the statement was defamatory of the plaintiff in the sense that:

    (i) it lowered him in the estimation of right thinking members of the society; or

    (ii) it exposed him to hatred, ridicule or contempt; or

    (iii) it injured his reputation in his office, trade or profession; or

    (iv) it injured his financial credit. To the above should be added

    (v) that the words were defamatory.

(a) Publication

In *Ugo* v *Okafor*,[13] the appellant a qualified homeopathy ran an Homeopathic Hospital at Enugu. In the course of his practice, he announced his feat of having produced a test - tube baby. This caused a lot of controversy in Nigeria. The 1st respondent thereafter issued a release, which was carried by the 2nd respondent in its *Daily Times* of 15th June, 1985. The publication read:

> The Homeopath Medical Association of Nigeria has disowned the controversial test - tube homeopathic doctor, Ernest Ugo, of the Calvary Foundation International of Enugu. In a release issued in Owerri, Imo State, on

---

[13] (1996) 3 NWLR (Pt 438) 542. See also *Nsirim* v *Nsirim* (1990) 3 NWLR (pt 138) 285; and *Douglas* v *Peterside* (1994) 3 NWLR (pt 330) 37

Thursday, the Association said that Dr. Ugo has never been, and is not *homeopath*! Addressing Newsmen at the Concord Hotel, Owerri, the national president of the association, Dr. M. O. Okafor, said that Dr. Ugo was not registered by the association nor was he recognised as qualified homeopath.

The appellant alleged that the publication defamed him and he sued the respondents claiming ₦100, 000.00 as damages for libel. The case was tried on the pleadings at the end of which the high court held that although the publication was defamatory of the appellant, there was no proof of publication of the defamatory matter in that it was not proved that one person other than the appellant read the defamatory matter. The case was thus dismissed. The court of Appeal, allowing the appeal held *inter alia*:

> By 'publication' is meant the making known of the defamatory matter to some persons other than the person of whom it is written. In order to succeed in an action for defamation, a plaintiff must prove that the libel or slander has been published, that is communicated to some person or persons other than the plaintiff himself.

On proof of publication of libel in a book or newspaper, the court held:

> it is not necessary in all cases to prove that the libellous matter was actually brought to the notice of some third party. If it is made a matter of reasonable inference that such was the fact, a *prima facie* case of publication will be established. This is particularly so when a book, magazine or newspaper containing a libel is sold by the defendant. Thus, a libel in any such documents like a book, magazine, or a newspaper or a post card (posted) is *prima facie* evidence of

publication by the proprietor, editor, publisher and printer and any person who sells or distributes it. Where the material is produced to the court by the National Library of Nigeria that will be a clear evidence that it was published to a third party.[14]

It should be pointed out that every repetition of a defamatory statement is a fresh publication and creates a fresh cause of action. An innocent disseminer is not liable except where he is negligent.[15]

(b) The defamatory statement must refer to the plaintiff

It has to be shown that the defamatory statement refers to the plaintiff. In *Dalumo* v *The Sketch Publishing Co. Ltd.*,[16] it was held thus:

it is an essential element of the cause of action for defamation that the words complained of should be published of the plaintiff.... It is not necessary that the words should refer to the plaintiff by name. Provided that the words could be understood by reasonable people to refer to him, and this is the test in every case, it is sufficient. As the law stands, the test of whether words that do not specifically name a plaintiff refer to him or not is this; are the words such as, reasonably in the circumstances, would lead persons who knew the plaintiff to believe that he was the person referred to?[17]

---

[14] At pg. 561. See also *Awoniyi* v *Registered Trustee of the Rosicrucian (AMORC)* (1990) 6 NWLR (pt 154) 42: *Fawehinmi* v *Akilu* (1994) 6 NWLR (pt 351) 387 and *Ajakaiye* v *Okandeji* (1972) 1SC 92.

[15] See *Awolowo* v *Kingsway Stores Ltd.* (1968) 2 All NLR 217

[16] (1972) 1 ALL NLR 130

[17] At pg. 568

This can be determined by the use of initials, nickname, office or post, a photograph, drawing or verbal description. In *Bakare* v *Olumide*,[18] it was held that the plaintiff who was a stevedoring and general contractor as well as a traditional ruler, was sufficiently identified by a cartoon closely resembling him and by reference to the exploitation of dockworkers which accompanied an article wherein the author attacked the alleged greed, corruption and debauchery of "the men of means in Nigeria."

Where the defamatory words relate to a whole class of persons an individual member of that class cannot sue except the class is small and ascertainable and the statement should be capable of referring to each and every member of that class. In *Knuppfer* v *London Express Newspaper Ltd.*,[19] Lord Porter said: "No doubt it is true to say that a class cannot be defamed as a class, nor can an individual be defamed by a general reference to the class which he belongs."

Furthermore, in *Eastwood* v *Homes*,[20] Willes J. said: "If a man wrote that all lawyers were thieves, no particular lawyer could sue him unless there was something to point to the particular individual."

(c) The defamatory words must convey a defamatory meaning to those to whom it was published

The determination of whether the defamatory words convey a defamatory meaning to those to whom it was published is

---

[18] (1969) 2 ALL NLR 321. See also *The Service Press Ltd.* v *Azikiwe* (1951) 14 WACA 176.
[19] (1944) A. C. 116.
[20] (1858) 1F & F 347 at 349

through the eye of a reasonable man in the circumstance. In *Sketch* v *Ajagbemokeferi*,[21] it was held that:

> In an action for defamation, the test of reasonableness is the guiding and directing test for the court in its function of deciding whether to hold that under the circumstances in which the words complained of are published, reasonable person to whom the publication was made would understand them in a defamatory sense. Thus in determining whether the words are capable of a defamatory meaning, the judge must construe the words according to the fair and natural meaning which would be given them by reasonable persons of ordinary intelligence and will not consider what persons settling themselves to work to deduce some unusual meaning might succeed in extracting from them.

In *Esika* v *Medolu*,[22] it was held that a person's reputation is not based on the good opinion he has of himself but the estimation in which the others held him.

The defamatory words may be an innuendo. Innuendoes are of two types (1) true or legal innuendo - the words used are not defamatory on their face but persons having special knowledge of some facts to whom the words are published may know that the words refer to the plaintiff.[23] In the case of (2) false or popular innuendo - the words are defamatory in themselves without extrinsic facts.[24]

---

[21] *Supra.* See also *Okolo* v *Midwest Newspaper Corporation* (1977) 1 SC 33; *Okafor* v *Ikeanyi* (1973) 3-4 SC 99 and *Dina* v *New Nigerian Newspaper Ltd.* (1986) 2 NWLR (pt 22) 353.

[22] *Supra.* See *Nsirim* v *Nsirim* (1990) 3 NWLR (pt 138) 285.

[23] See *Akintola* v *Anyiam* (1961) 1 ALL NLR 508

[24] See *Mutual Aid Society Ltd.* v *Akerele* (1962) LL.R 46

(d) The defamatory statement must lower the plaintiff in society or expose him to hatred, ridicule or contempt or injure his reputation in his office, trade, profession or financial credit.

This was clearly stated in *Esika* v *Medolu*.[25] The basis of defamation is the complaint by the plaintiff that he has been injured in respect of his reputation, trade, profession or financial credit or that he has been lowered in the estimation of the members of the public.[26]

(e) The words must be defamatory

The court must determine whether the words are defamatory. The determination of this is objective. Adefarasin J. in *Omo–Osagie* v *Okutubo*,[27] said:

> The judge..... has to consider what is the natural and ordinary meaning in which these words would be understood by reasonable men to whom they were published. In determining whether the words are capable of a defamatory meaning, the judge should construe the words according to the fair and natural meaning which would be given to them by reasonable persons of ordinary intelligence who are neither unusually suspicious nor unusually naïve.

Defences

Persons who can be referred to as innocent disseminators such as booksellers who sell books which contain libellous material,

---

[25] *Supra.*

[26] See *Izuogu* v *Emuwa* (1991) 4 NWLR (pt 183) 78.

[27] (1969) 2 ALL NLR 175 at 179

newspaper vendors, libraries or museum may raise the defence of innocence where it is shown that;

(i) at the time they disseminated the material they did not know that it contained libellous matter and

(ii) it was not due to negligence on their part in not discovering the libel contained in the article, newspaper or book.

The popular defences are -
(a) justification
(b) fair comment
(c) absolute privilege and
(d) qualified privilege.

Some of these defences are now regulated by statute.

(a) Justification

This defence relates to the truth of the statement. By this, the defendant asserts that although he has truly published the alleged defamatory words, but he has spoken or published the truth. In *Iwuoha* v *Okoroike*,[28] it was held thus:

> A plea of justification means that the words were true and the plea covers not only the bare statements of fact in the alleged libel, but also any imputation which the words in their context may be taken to convey.

Furthermore, in *McPherson* v *Daniels*,[29] Littledale J. said: "the law will not permit a man to recover damages in respect of

---

[28] (1996) 2 NWLR (pt 429) 231, See also *Obakpolar* v *Oyefeso* (1997) 6 NWLR (pt 508) 256; Section 377 of the Criminal Code makes truth a defence to a charge of defamation.

[29] (1829) 1 Q. B. & C 263 at 272

an injury to a character which he either does not, or ought not to possess."

Section 11 of the Defamation Law of Oyo State provides that in an action for libel or slander in respect of words containing two or more distinct charges against the plaintiff, a defence of justification shall not fail by reason only that the truth of every charge is not proved if the words not proved to be true do not materially injure the plaintiff's reputation having regard to the truth of the remaining charges. In *Iwuoha* v *Okoroike*,[30] it was held that where in an action for defamation the defence raises a plea of justification, the procedure to follow is for the plaintiff first to tender the document complained of and then give formal evidence of the libel after which the defendant leads evidence in support of his plea of justification and the plaintiff may then give evidence in rebuttal.[31]

(b) Fair comment

The basis of this defence is that the statement is a fair comment on a matter of public interest. It is felt that honest criticism ought to be allowed as it is done in any civilised society since this is necessary and indispensable for the efficient working of any public institution or office. In *Ugo* v *Okafor*,[32] it was held that the defence of fair comment is open to every member of the public. In order to succeed, the defendant must show

(a) that the matter is of public interest

(b) that the words complained about the plaintiff are comment

---

[30] *Supra.*

[31] See also *Pedro* v *Orafidiya* (1975) 1 NMLR 336 (a) (1996) NWLR (pt 438) 542

[32] See also *Ugo* v *Okafor supra; Sketch Publication Co.* v *Ajagbemokeferi* (1989) 1 NWLR (pt 100) 678.

(c) that the facts on which the comment is founded or based are true; and

(d) that the comment on the facts is true.

For a comment to be fair, the following conditions must be satisfied:

(i) it must be based on facts truly stated

(ii) it must not contain imputations of corrupt or dishonourable motives on the person whose conduct or work is criticised save in so far as such imputations are warranted by the facts

(iii) it must be the honest expression of the writer's real intention. Mere exaggeration or even gross exaggeration would not necessarily make the comment unfair.

A roll-up plea is usually taken to be a plea of both justification and fair comment. By it, the defendant tries to show that the facts on which he based his comments are true. Section 12 of the Defamation Law of Oyo State provides thus:

> in an action for libel or slander in respect of words consisting partly of allegations of fact and partly of expressions of opinion a defence of fair comment shall not fail by reason only that the truth of every allegation of fact is not proved if the expression of opinion is fair comment having regard to such of the facts alleged or referred to in the words complained of as proved.

In *Sketch* v *Ajagbemokeferi*,[33] the court held that in a rolled-up plea, which is the essence of a defence of fair comment, the

---

[33] *Supra.*

jury, or the judge, as the case may be, must make a finding of the following:

(a) are the words complained of statements of fact or expression of opinion or partly one and partly the other?
(b) in so far as they are statements of fact, are such statements of true facts?
(c) in so far as they are expressions of opinion, do such expressions of opinion exceed the limits of fair comment?

Distinction between fair comment and justification

The element of truth in the defence of fair comment does not make it a defence of justification. A defence of justification means that the libel is true not only in its allegation of facts, but also in any comment made therein. On the other hand, in the defence of fair comment, the defendant does not take upon himself the burden of showing that the comments are true. If the facts are truly stated with regard to a matter of public interest, the defendant will succeed if the court is satisfied that the comments are fairly and honestly made.

(c) Absolute privilege

Absolute privilege is a complete defence to defamation. It may be used as a defence in cases of proceedings in the Legislative House or in a court of law or where public policy demands that persons should be able to have free discussion on issues with absolute freedom and without fear. In *Ojeme* v *Punch (Nig.) Ltd*,[34] it was held that: "a fair and absolute report in newspaper, or proceedings held before any court exercising judicial

---

[34] (1996) 1 NWLR (pt 427) 701

authority if published contemporaneously with the proceedings is absolutely privileged."

It was thus held that for a newspaper report of judicial proceedings to be privileged, it must be a fair and accurate account of what took place in court.[35] Section 378 of the Criminal Code deals with instances when a defamatory matter is absolutely privileged.

(d) Qualified privilege

Both absolute and qualified privilege protect persons who make defamatory statements in circumstances where the common convenience and welfare of society is in issue and demands such protection. While absolute privilege is confined to instances stated above, qualified privilege is wide enough to cover all cases where public interest demands that truth be told.

In *Ogoja L.G.* v *Offoboche*,[36] the court held that:

> In general, an action lies for the malicious publication of statements which are false in fact, and injurious to the character of another, and the law considers such publication as malicious, unless it is fairly made by a person in the discharge of some public or private duty, whether legal or moral, or in the conduct of his own affairs, in matters where his interest is concerned. In such cases, the occasion prevents the inference of malice which the law draws from unauthorised communications, and affords a qualified defence depending on the absence of actual malice. If fairly warranted by any reasonable occasion or exigency, and honestly made, such communications are protected for the common convenience and welfare of society.

---

[35] See also *Majekodunmi* v *Olopade* (1963) NMLR 12; *Chartterton* v *Secretary of State for India* (1895) 2 Q.B. 189; *Royal Acquarium* v *Parkinson* (1892) I.Q.B. 431.

[36] (1996) 7 NWLR (pt 458) 52

In *African Newspapers Ltd.* v *Ciroma*,[37] the Court of Appeal held that the essential element of qualified privilege is reciprocity of interest as the facts relied on by the maker must be true since mere belief is insufficient.

Instances of qualified privilege include:

i.   Statements made in the performance of a legal, moral or social duty.[38]

ii.   Statements made in self-defence- This may happen in the defence of one's trade or name.[39]

iii. Statements made between parties having a common interest. This may be pecuniary or professional.[40]

iv.   Statements made to the proper authorities in order to obtain redress for public or private grievances.[41]

v.   Fair and accurate reports of proceedings in the Legislative House.[42]

vi.   Fair and accurate reports of judicial proceedings.[43]

vii. Comments privileged by statute.[44]

Section 379 of the Criminal Code states instances when qualified privilege may be raised as a defence.

---

[37] (1996) 1 NWLR (pt 423) 156 . See also *Atoyebi* v *Odudu* (1990) 6 NWLR (pt 157) 384, *African Newspapers Ltd.* v *Coker* (1973) 1 NWLR 386. See further *Ogoja* v *Offoboche* (1996) 7 NWLR (pt 458) 52.

[38] *Economides* v *Thomopulos* (1956) NLR 7, See also *Ayoola* v *Olajire* (1977) 3 CC HCJ 315.

[39] *Osborn* v *Boulter* (1930) 2 K.B. 226

[40] *Obikoya* v *Ezenwa* (1973) 1 All NLR (pt II) 64

[41] *Dikey* v *Odeniyi* (1960) NWLR 102, See also *Ajala* v *Showumi* (1977) 1 CC HCJ 25.

[42] *Oweh* v *Amalgamated Press of Nigeria Ltd.* (1957) 1 LL.R 6

[43] *Omo Osagie* v *Okutubo* (1969) 2 All NLR 175. See for example section 16 of the Defamation Law of Oyo State.

[44] See for example section 16 of the Defamation Law of Oyo State.

Malice

Malice may destroy the defence of fair comment or qualified privilege. By this is meant the use of a privileged occasion for an improper purpose. Abbott J. put the matter thus in *Oweh* v *Amalgamated Press of Nigeria Ltd*:[45]

> actual malice does not necessarily mean personal spite of ill-will and may exist even though there be no spite or desire for vengeance in the ordinary sense. Any indirect motive other than a sense of duty is what the law calls malice. Malice means making use of the occasion for some indirect purpose.

Apart from these substantive defences, the following may affect an action brought by the plaintiff –

(a) death of the plaintiff or defendant
(b) consent of the plaintiff. The maxim is *volenti non fit injuria*
(c) Statute of limitation. This is because nothing can call the court into activity, but conscience, good faith and reasonable diligence. Where these are wanting the court is passive and does nothing.
(d) *Res judicata*
(e) Accord and satisfaction. This may be achieved by publication of a correction of the defamatory words or an apology for the publication.

---

[45] (1956) LL.R. 6

In *Harbror* v *Eronini*,[46] Bairaiman J. said:

> In libel cases, an apology withdrawing whatever imputations contained in the article complained of and stating that the writer "regrets" whatever inconvenience or embarrassment they have caused the plaintiff is an admission that the words complained of bear defamatory meaning.

Assessment of damages

In *Concord Press Ltd.* v *Obijo*,[47] the court held that in assessing damages in libel cases, the court is entitled to take into consideration:
  (a) the conduct of the plaintiff,
  (b) the plaintiff's position and standing
  (c) the nature of the libel
  (d) the mode and extent of publication
  (e) the absence or refusal of any retraction or apology and
  (f) the whole conduct of the defendant from the time when the libel was published down to the very moment of the verdict.

It should be noted that it is crucial in a case of libel or slander to prove publication. This must be pleaded and proved. This is because in this area of the law it is publication that gives a case its cause of action.[48]

It could thus be said that the philosophy behind the recognition of defamation is the need to protect persons from

---

[46] (1986) NSCC 420

[47] (1990) 7 NWLR (pt 162) 303. See also *Dina* v *New Nigerian Newspapers Ltd. Supra.*

[48] See *Ugbomor* v *Hadomeh* (1997) 9 NWLR (pt 520) 307. See also *Giwa* v *Ajayi* (1993) 5 NWLR (pt 294) 423.

unjustifiable accusation and imputation or as Iguh eloquently put it in *Cross River State Newspapers Corporation* v *Oni*,[49]

> it is not the law that one's general character or reputation must transparently be stainless, unimpeachable and without any blemish whatsoever before one can successfully maintain an action for defamation.

---

[49] (1995) 1 NWLR (pt 371) 270.

5

Contempt of court

One offence that a journalist may commit in the performance of his duties is that of contempt of court especially where the issue has something to do with the court of law or the order of a court of law.

Contempt of court or in its Latin expression *contemptus curie* is difficult to define. This is because it is manifold in its aspect.[1] Notwithstanding the definitional problem, it may be described as any conduct which tends to bring into disrespect, scorn or disrepute the authority and administration of the law or which tends to interfere with and/or prejudice litigants and/or their witnesses in the course of litigation.[2] Therefore, any act done or writing published which is calculated to bring a court or a judge into contempt or to lower his authority or to interfere with the due course of justice or the lawful process of the court is contempt.[3]

It needs be pointed out that when a judge exercises his power of punishment for contempt of court, he does so not out of any desire to vindicate his personality, the law of defamation provides adequate remedy in this regard, but out of desire to

---

[1] Oswald on *Contempt* 3rd ed. P.5.

[2] See *Franklin O. Atake* v *The Attorney-General of the Federation & anor.* (1982) 11 S.C. 153 at 175 - 176.

[3] See *Adeniji-Adele* v *Ogbe* (1989) 9 NWLR (part 567) 650. See also *Awobokun* v *Adeyemi* (1968) NMLR 289, *Ezeji* v *Ike* (1997) 2 NWLR (part 486) 206.

preserve and protect the authority of the court in the interest of the general public. Thus, in *Mclead* v *St. Aubyn*,[4] Lord Morris said:

> The power summarily to commit for contempt of court is considered necessary for the proper administration of justice. It is not to be used for the vindication of the judge as a person. He must resort to action for libel or criminal information. Committal for contempt of court is a weapon to be used sparingly and always with reference to the interests of the administration of justice.[5]

Thus, it could be said that what the law of contempt seeks is an assurance that nothing is done to undermine the authority of the court or administration of justice. As Lord Hardwicke pointed out "there cannot be anything of greater consequence than to keep the streams of justice clear and pure, that parties may proceed with safety both to themselves and their characters."

Basis of the power of the court to punish for contempt

The power of the court to punish for contempt of court had its initial authority from the "inherent powers" of a superior court of law to punish for contempt. In relation to Nigeria, It is not enough to say this. It is therefore necessary to look at various statutes for the authority bestowed on the courts to punish for contempt..

Section 133 of chapter XIII of Part III to the Schedule to the Criminal Code Act or simply section 133 of the criminal code

---

[4] (1880) A.C. 549 at 561.
[5] This decision was approved and followed in *Godwin Mogbeyi Boyo* v *The Attorney-General of Mid Western State* (1971) 1 All NLR 342 at 352 - 353.

provides for instances when a person can be punished for contempt of court. It states:

Any person who -
(1) within the premises in which any judicial proceeding is being had or taken, or within the precincts of the same, shows disrespect in speech or manner, to or with reference to such proceeding, or any person before whom such proceeding is being had or taken; or
(2) having been called upon to give evidence in a judicial proceeding, fails to attend or, having attended, refused to be sworn or to make an affirmation, or having been sworn or affirmed, refuses without lawful excuse to answer a question or to produce a document or prevaricates, or remains in the room in which such proceeding is being had or taken, after the witnesses have been ordered to leave such room; or
(3) causes an obstruction or disturbances in the course of a judicial proceeding; or
(4) while a judicial proceeding is pending, makes use of any speech or writing, misrepresenting such proceeding, or capable of prejudicing any person in favour of or against any party to such proceeding, or calculated to lower the authority of any person before whom such proceeding is being had or taken; or
(5) publishes a report of the evidence taken in any judicial proceeding which has been directed to be held in private; or
(6) attempts wrongly to interfere with or influence a witness in a judicial proceeding, either before or after he has given evidence, in connection with such evidence; or
(7) dismisses a servant because he has given evidence on behalf of a certain party to a judicial proceeding; or
(8) retakes possession of land from any person who has recently obtained possession by a writ of court; or

(9) commits any other act of intentional disrespect to any judicial proceeding, or to any person before whom such proceeding is being had or taken is guilty of a simple offence, and liable to imprisonment for three months.

Apart from the specific situations provided for in section 133(1) - (8), section 133(9) states the general power of the court to punish for contempt. Thus if any situation arises which cannot be referred to any of the first eight sub-sections, section 133(9) can be invoked to punish any person whose conduct has the colour of contempt.

It needs to be considered whether apart from the provision of the criminal code, any other law of imperative or high authority recognises the offence of contempt of court. Section 22(10) of the 1963 Constitution provided:

No person shall be convicted of a criminal offence unless that offence is defined and the penalty therefore is prescribed in a written law. Provided that nothing in this subsection shall prevent a court of record from punishing any person for contempt of itself notwithstanding that the act or omission constituting the contempt is not defined in a written law and the penalty therefore is not so prescribed.

Section 33(12) of the 1979 Constitution which is similar to section 22(10) of the 1963 Constitution does not contain the portion of the 1963 Constitution which stated that

provided that nothing in this sub-section shall prevent a court of record from punishing any person for contempt of itself notwithstanding that the act or omission constituting the contempt is not defined in a written law and the penalty therefore is not so prescribed.

Notwithstanding this however, there are other provisions in the 1979 Constitution that preserve the power of the court to punish for contempt. For example section 6(6)(a) of the 1979 Constitution provides:

> The judicial powers vested in accordance with the foregoing provisions of this section (a) shall extend, notwithstanding anything to the contrary in this constitution, to all inherent powers and sanctions of a court of law.[6]

When it is remembered that, historically, the power of the court to punish for contempt derives from the inherent nature of the judicial system, then it could be concluded that section 6(6)(a) of the 1979 Constitution is an enactment of the power of the court in this regard.

Furthermore, section 6 of the Criminal Code Act provides thus:

> Nothing in this Ordinance or in this Code shall affect the authority of courts of record to punish a person summarily[7] for the offence commonly known as contempt of court; but so that a person cannot be so punished and also punished under the provisions of the code for the same act or omission.[7]

It could therefore be concluded that the power of the court to punish is not only a matter of inference from the inherent power of the court to do justice or that derived from the criminal code *per se* but it is constitutionally clothed with necessary toga of authority even though a full trial may not occur. Justification for

---

[6] Emphasis added.

[7] Emphasis added.

this was summarily put by Stephenson L.J. in *Balogh* v *St. Albans Crown Court*,[8]

> The power of a superior court to commit (or attach) a contemnor to prison without charge or trial is very ancient, very necessary, but very unusual, if not indeed unique. It is as old as the courts themselves and it is necessary for the performance of their function of administering justice, whether they exercise criminal or civil jurisdiction.
>
> If they are to do justice they need power to administer it without interference or affront, as well as to enforce their own orders and to punish those who insult or obstruct them directly or indirectly in the performance of their duty or misbehave in such a manner as to weaken or lower the dignity and authority of law ...[9]

Now that it is established that a person can be charged to court or imprisoned for contempt of court, it can now be determined the types of contempt we have.

Forms of contempt

There are two types of contempt. They are (1) criminal contempt and (ii) civil or non-criminal contempt. In *Hart* v *Hart*,[10] it was held that contempt of court is either criminal or civil. (a) It is criminal when it consists of interference with the administration of law thus impeding and preventing the course of justice (b) It is civil when it consists of disobedience to the judgement, orders

---

[8] (1975) 1 Q.B. 75 at 88.

[9] (1990) 1 NWLR (pt 126) 276.

[10] (1990) 1 NWLR (pt 126). See also *Mobil Oil (Nig.) Ltd.* v *Asan* (1995) 8 NWLR (part 430) 322; *Adeniji Adele* v *Ogbe* (1998) 9 NWLR (pt 567) 650.

or other processes of the court resulting or involving private injury. In *Kolbian (Nig.) Ltd.* v *Lawrence Bros*,[11] it was held that every court has inherent powers to punish summarily any act of contempt committed before it i.e. *in facie curia*, but any contempt committed, *ex facie curia,* i.e. outside the court, cannot be so punished.

The above discussion raises two issues. The first is that contempt of court may either be criminal or civil. The second is that contempt is either *in faciae curiae* or *ex-faciae curiae* the trial is summary and no pleas are taken. The contemnor is dealt with instantly and must not be put in the witness box to be cross examined by the trial judge. In the case of contempt not committed in the face of the court, a charge and a plea are necessary and the contemnor is entitled to a fair hearing of the case against him. Thus, it could be said that after determining the nature of contempt, it still has to be determined whether it is contempt *in faciae curiae* or *ex faciae curiae* in order to know the appropriate procedure to adopt.[12]

Procedure for committal for contempt

The determination of the appropriate procedure to adopt in punishing for contempt was in a state of flux until the decision of the Supreme Court in *Atake* v *The Attorney -General of the Federation*.[13] The Court of Appeal in *Dibia* v *Igwe & 14 Ors*,[14] stated the procedure thus:

---

[11] (1990) 3 NWLR (pt 138) 356 at 361.
[12] Hon. Justice O. Onalaja, "Contempt of Court" Lecture Notes No. 2 Continuing Legal Education Association (Nigeria) CLEA(N) delivered on 18th November, 1989.
[13] *Supra*
[14] (1998) 9 NWLR (pt 564) 78 at 83.

The offence of contempt of court can basically be divided into two categories namely (a). contempt *in facie curiae* otherwise known as contempt in the face of the court, and (b) contempt *ex facie curiae* or contempt outside the court. In respect of (a) the contemnor can be tried summarily. This means that the trial judge who wishes to deal summarily with a case of contempt in the face of the court, should or would put the accused in the dock and ask him to show cause why he should not be committed for contempt. It must be emphasised here that the accused should not be put in the witness box. For putting the accused in the witness box, is tantamount to compelling him to give evidence as this clearly offends against the provisions of Section 33 (1) of the 1979 Constitution of the Federal Republic of Nigeria as amended which says that no person who is tried for a criminal offence shall be compelled to give evidence at the trial.[15]

The authorities are agreed that a contempt in the face of the court is dealt with summarily. In applying the summary procedure certain requirements must be observed. These include asking the alleged contemnor to go into the dock, stating his offence specifically and distinctly to him and asking him to show cause from the dock why he should not be committed for contempt of court.

In the case of (b), that is contempt committed outside the court (*ex facie curiae*) the proper procedure of apprehension or arrest, charge and prosecution etc. must be applied and followed. In such a situation, the case should and must be tried by another judge.[15]

The question may be asked, what is the test for determining culpability.

---

[15] See *Agbachom* v *The State* (1970) 1 All N.L.R. 69; *Deduwa & Ors* v *The State* (1975) 1 All N.L.R. (pt.1) 1; *Atake* v *A.G. of the Federation* (1981) 11 SC 153.

In *Atake* v *The Attorney-General of the Federation*,[16] Idigbe J.S.C. held that the test for determining what constitutes contempt of court in the face of the court is subjective. He pointed out that:

> It is for this reason that the court which decides to deal with the offence does not require any application by a third party or, for that matter, an affidavit as it must have in matters of contempt NOT in *curiae facie* setting out the facts which ought to enable it to arrive at the decision whether or not an alleged contemnor is *de facto* and *de jure* in contempt of court.

What is the *mens rea* required particularly in relation to contempt *in facie curiae*? The Supreme court in the case of *Atake* v *The Attorney-General of the Federation*,[17] held that this does not matter to the court. The intention of the contemnor may be relevant to the degree of punishment.

What acts constitute contempt of court?

It is very difficult to determine in the abstract acts which constitute contempt of court. Notwithstanding the itemisation of acts which may constitute contempt of court and the general provision in section 133 (9) of the Criminal Code, it cannot be stated with precision acts which constitute contempt of court but as stated in *Atake* v *The Attorney-General of the Federation*,[18] the power is not granted to vindicate the personality of the judge. The best approach is to look at decided cases. But before this is embarked upon, it is necessary to bear in mind the

[16] *Supra* at pg. 195

[17] *Supra* at pp. 179 - 180

[18] *Supra* at p. 194.

opinion of Wilmot J. in a judgment he never delivered in *The King* v *Almon*,[19]

> Contempt of court involves two ideas: contempt of their power, and contempt of their authority. The word "authority" is frequently used to express both the right of declaring the law..... and for enforcing obedience to it in which sense it is equivalent to the word power: but by the word "authority" I do not mean the coercive power of the judges, but the deference and respect which is paid to them and their acts, from an opinion of their acts, from an opinion of their justice and integrity.

> Livy uses it according to my idea of the word, in his character of Evander: *Authoritate magis quam imperio pollebat*: It is not *'imperium'*, it is not coercive power of the court: but it is homage and obedience to the court, from the opinion of the qualities of the judges who compose it; it is a confidence in their wisdom and integrity, that the power they have is applied to the purpose for which it was deposited in their hands; that authority acts as the great auxilliary of their power, and for that reason the constitution gives them this compedious mode of proceeding against all who shall endeavour to impair and abate it...... In *Parashburam Shamdasani* v *The King Emperor*,[20] Lord Goddard said:

> Their Lordships would again emphasise, what has often been said before, that this summary power of punishing for contempt should be used sparingly and only in serious cases, it is a power which a court must of necessity possess. Its usefulness depends on the wisdom and restraint with which it is exercised, and to use it to suppress methods of advocacy

---

[19] (1765) Wil. 243 at 256 - 257 or 97 E.R. 100.
[20] (1945) A.C. 264.

which are merely offensive is to use it for a purpose for
which it was never intended.

It is not every act of discourtesy to the court by counsel that
amounts to contempt.[21]

In *R* v *Thomas Horatius Jackson*,[22] on the 29th October,
1925, Thomas Horatius Jackson, proprietor and editor of a
newspaper called the *Lagos Weekend Record*, appeared before
the Supreme Court on an order requiring him to show cause why
he should not be committed for contempt of court in respect of
articles published in his newspaper which cast grave aspersions
against the integrity and impartiality of the Judges of the court.

In September 1925, the Acting Chief Justice gave a judgment
in favour of the defendants in an action in which Eshugbayi was
the plaintiff and the officer administering the Government and
Chief Secretary were defendants. In the issues of the *Lagos
Weekly Record* of September 19th and 26th, Jackson who, as his
counsel stated before the court, was a strong protagonist of the
cause of the plaintiff in that case, wrote and published two
articles, the first under the caption "A Great Constitutional
Issue" and the second under the caption "The Dangers of the
Judicial System of Nigeria" referring to the decision of the
Acting Chief Justice in the case, and alleging with reference to
that case and to other cases in which the Government has been
concerned that the Judges of this court were under the subjection
of the Executive, and will not and dare not give a decision
unfavourable to the Government, and have been compelled to
invent plausible arguments in order to be able to record
decisions compatible with the wishes of the Executive. These

---

[21] See *Izuora* v *The Queen* (1953) 13 WACA 313
[22] (1899) A.C. 549.

articles were said to contain scandalous reflection upon the integrity of the court and that the publication of these articles constituted a gross contempt of court. Combe C.J. delivering the judgment of the court held:

> This man Thomas Horatius Jackson, using the paper of which he is the editor and proprietor as his instrument, has sought to persuade the public that no confidence can be placed in this court since the judges are afraid to give decisions which might not meet with the approval of the Executive. These wicked aspersions on the integrity of Judges of this court must, through the medium of this newspaper, reach many of the less advanced members of the communities of the Colony and Protectorate who cannot be expected to appraise at their true value statements made in the leading articles of that newspaper. Hence incalculable damage may be done by the publication of the articles which have given rise to these proceedings. Indeed I cannot imagine any greater evil which could befall the people of this colony and protectorate than that Jackson should succeed in his efforts to render this court contemptible in the eyes of the public......... it would be my duty to commit Jackson to prison for a very considerable time.

In *R* v *Commissioner of Police of the Metropolis*,[23] a lawyer, Mr. Quinn Hogg was held not guilty of contempt in respect of an article he wrote. He strongly criticised the English Court of Appeal. In this case, Lord Denning re-affirmed the view that the power of contempt must be exercised sparingly.

He remarked as follows:

---

[23] (1968) 2 Q.B. 150.

Let me say at once that we will never use this jurisdiction as a means to uphold our own dignity. That must rest on surer foundations. Nor will we use it to suppress those who speak against us. We do not fear criticism, nor do we resent it for there is something far more important at stake. It is no less than freedom of speech itself.

In *Dibia* v *Igwe*,[24] on the 4th of June, 1996, the 14th respondent herein wrote a letter to the learned trial judge, the contents of which the learned trial judge held to be contemptuous and in consequence ordered the arrest of the 14th respondent and proceeded to try him summarily for contempt.

The 14th respondent, on being asked to show cause why he should not be committed to prison for contempt of court, alleged that he wrote the offending letter on the instruction of the appellant, Newton Okoro. The appellant denied the allegation but told the court that the 14th respondent only offered to assist him in his case before the court but did not however disclose the nature of the assistance. The learned trial judge believed the 14th respondent and in consequence committed both the appellant and the 14th respondent to prison for 30 days for contempt of court. On appeal to the Court of Appeal, it was held that the procedure adopted by the learned trial judge was wrong since the contempt was committed *ex facie curiae*, the trial judge should not have proceeded summarily against him. The court quoted with approval, the judgment of the Supreme Court in *Ene Oku* v *The State*,[25] where it was held as follows:

---

[24] (1998) 9 NWLR (pt. 564); See also *Bonnie* v *Gold* (1996) 8 NWLR (pt. 465) 230.

[25] (1970) 1 All NLR 60; See also *Agbachom* v *The State* (1970) 1 All NLR 69; *Deduwa* v *The State* (1975) 1 All NLR (pt 1) 1. Other cases dealing with contempt of court include *R* v *Ojukoko* (1926) 7 NLR 60; *Re Onagoruwa*; *Izuora* v *The Queen* (1953) A.C. 327; *Governor of Lagos State* v *Ojukwu* (1986) 1 NWLR (pt. 18) 621 and *Ibrahim* v *Emein* (1996) 2 NWLR (pt 430) 322.

> Where contempt of court is punished '*brevi manu*' in court no warrant is necessary for the apprehension of the offender as he is always in court and the contempt is stated to have been committed '*coram judice*' but in other cases the proper procedure of apprehension of arrest, charge, prosecution etc. must be followed.

The law of contempt attempts to balance the recognised freedom of speech and/or expression and the need to maintain the integrity of the courts and administration of justice. The press performing its duties must endeavour to balance the interest of having to inform the public on pertinent issues and in ensuring that nothing is done to clog or bring to ridicule the administration of justice. A journalist should be careful in reporting issues which are subjudice.

In *Attorney General* v *Times Newspapers Ltd*,[26] the court held that when litigation is pending and actively in suit before the court, no one shall comment on it in such a way that there is a real and substantial danger of prejudice to the trial of the action, as for instance by influencing the judge, the jurors, or the witnesses, or even by prejudicing mankind in general against a party to the cause. The court also maintained that the interests of the parties are however to be weighed against the public interest such that where the issues raised by the litigation are of national concern, public comment on those issues is permissible provided that it is fair and based on an accurate statement of the facts. In *Waller Steiner* v *Moir*,[27] the court held that the issuance of a writ cannot be used as a pretext for preventing the discussion of matters of public interest on the ground that those matters are subjudice. Accordingly where a company's affairs are the

---

[26] (1973) 1 All E.R. 815.
[27] (1974) 3 All E.R. 217.

subject of legal proceedings discussion of those affairs is not contempt of court.

6

Sedition

One of the cornerstones upon which a virile society is built is freedom of expression. Thus, most constitutions provide for freedom of expression so that debate on public issues may be un-inhibited and such debate may well include vehement, caustic and sometimes unpleasant sharp attacks on government and public officials.[1]

In line with the above, section 36 of the 1979 Constitution provides that every person shall be entitled to freedom of expression, including freedom to hold opinions and to receive and impart ideas and information without interference.[2]

The criminal code of Nigeria deals with the offence of sedition. At a glance, it would seem that this provision runs counter to freedom of expression but it was pointed out in *Francis* v *Chief of Police*[3] that:

> the statutory requirement for the control of the loud speakers did not violate the constitutionally entrenched right of free

---

[1] *New York Times* v *Sullivan*, 376 U.I. 254 at 270. See generally T.O. Elias, *Nigerian Press Law* (Evans). 1969.

[2] The 1979 Constitution of Nigeria became operational on the 1st day of October, 1979 when civil rule was restored. The military however took over government again in December 1983, part of the constitution was suspended. The transition to civil rule programme is on course. It is hoped that the military will disengage on 29 May 1999. It should be stated that section 36 of the 1979 Constitution has not been abrogated. Decisions under the 1979 Constitution will definitely give focus to the provision on freedom of expression and the Press under the new Constitution.

[3] (1973) AC 761.

speech since such regulations were necessary in the interest of public order.

That this is the position can be seen from section 41(1) of the 1979 Constitution which provides that:

> nothing in sections 34, 35, 36, 37 and 38 of this constitution shall invalidate any law that is reasonably justifiable in a democratic society -
> (a) in the interest of defence, public safety, public order public morality or public health; or
> (b) for the purpose of protecting the rights and freedom of other persons.

The Criminal Code of Nigeria also recognises the offence of sedition. This could be found in sections 50, 51 and 52 of the Code. Section 51(1) of the criminal code provides that any person who:

> (a) does or attempts to do, or conspires with any person to do, any act with a seditious intention
> (b) utters any seditious words
> (c) imports any seditious publication, unless he has no reason to believe that it is seditious is guilty of this offence.

It is further provided that any person who without lawful excuse has in his possession any seditious publication shall be guilty of an offence. "seditious publication" and " seditious words" have been taken to mean publication or words having a seditious intention.

A person publishes anything if he makes it known to another and every time this is done a distinct offence is committed.

The mental element required for this offence to be committed is a seditious intention. This is defined in section 50(2) of the criminal code as an intention:

(a) to bring into hatred or contempt or to excite disaffection against the person of the president, or the Governor of a state, or the Government of the federation, or of any state thereof as by law established or against the administration of justice in Nigeria; or

(b) to excite the citizens or other inhabitants of Nigeria to attempt to procure the alteration, otherwise than by lawful means of any other matter in Nigeria as by law established; or

(c) to raise discontent or disaffection amongst the citizens or other inhabitants of Nigeria; or

(d) to promote feelings of ill-will and hostility between different classes of the population of Nigeria.

The recognition of this offence does not, in itself, mean that a person cannot comment on an issue of public interest. In *D.P.P. v Chike Obi*[4] the court held that:

> a person has a right to discuss any grievance, or criticise, canvass or censure acts of government and their public policy. He may even do this with a view to effecting a change in the party in power... what is not permitted is to criticise the government in such a malignant manner for such attacks by their very nature tend to affect the public peace.

A point of interest that has arisen from this discussion is the recognition of freedom to hold opinions and receive and impart ideas and information without interference. Yet the law recognises that it may be an offence where the government is

---

[4] (1961) 1 All NLR 186.

criticised in a malignant manner as to cause hatred or contempt or excite disaffection or raise discontent, ill-will or hostility. There must therefore, be a dividing line between the level of tolerance and culpability. This could be determined from decided cases. In *R. v Sullivan,*[5] Fitzgerald J. described sedition as a crime against society nearly allied to that of treason and that it frequently "precedes treason by a short interval." It is said to embrace "all those practices whether by word, deed or writing which are calculated to disturb the tranquillity of the state and lead against person to endeavour to subvert the government and the laws of the Empire."

Furthermore, the object of sedition is generally to induce discontent and insurrection and stir up opposition against the government as well as bring the administration of justice into contempt. It has the very tendency of subjecting the people to insurrection and hatred.[6]

Be that as it may, it is the position of our law that an act, speech or publication is not seditious under the code by reason only that it tends to show that the government has been misled or mistaken in any measure, or to point out errors or defects or to persuade the citizen of Nigeria to attempt to produce by lawful means the alteration of any matter in Nigeria as by law established or to point out, with a view to their removal, any matters which are producing or have a tendency to produce feelings of ill-will and enmity between different classes of the population in Nigeria. Thus, the right of the citizen to criticise the government in order to point out errors or mistakes is preserved. This is the effect of the second paragraph of section 50.

---

[5] (1886) 11 Cox C.C 44
[6] At pg. 59.

The question may be asked, what is the position of a publication that partly contains fair criticism and is partly seditious? In *Wallace Johnson* v *The king*,[7] it was pointed out that -

> questions will necessarily arise in every case as to the facts to which it is sought to apply these definitions. Fine distinctions may have to be drawn between facts which justify the conclusions that the intention of the person charged was to bring into hatred and contempt the government and facts which are consistent only with the view that the intention was no more than to point out errors or defects in Government.

It is a matter of construction. Thus is determining whether a publication is seditious, the whole publication will be considered and if it is found that the aspect containing seditious intention outweighs the fair comment, then the accused will be convicted of sedition. In *I. G. P.* v *Anagbogu*,[8] Bairamian J. pointed out that:

> he who writes an article with a seditious intention as defined in (a) to (d) cannot by including in the article criticism which is legitimate under (i) to (iv) be excused from a charge of writing a seditious article often enough a seditious article does contain parts which are not seditious. These parts do not excuse the article from being seditious.

It is not in all cases that the determination of whether a seditious intention existed before the publication will be an issue that can be expressly determined. Indeed, as a general rule, the

---

[7] 5 WACA 56 at p. 60.
[8] (1954) 21 NLR 26.

determination of seditious intention is a matter of inference from the manner in which the article is published. To publish to the world at large instead of confining publication to the appropriate person concerned with the matter may be suggestive of a seditious intention. In *Police* v *Ogidi*,[9] the accused sent a telegram to a Minister accusing customary courts of being creatures of a political party and of discriminating against opponents of that party. These views were published in the press. The court held that this latter action indicated a seditious intention. He was thus held liable.

It is the position of the law that words and phrases should be interpreted with regard to the prevailing situation. The court will therefore consider the surrounding circumstances in order to show the intention with which an article is published.

The law of sedition in Nigeria differs from the provisions of the law in other jurisdictions in one particular respect. In Nigeria, there is no need to prove that the accused did not have the intention of inciting people to violence. It has been established in the case of *R.* v *Wallace Johnson*[10] that "violence may well be, and no doubt often is, the result of wild and ill-considered words, but the code does not require proof from the words themselves of any intention to produce the result."

Nigeria is not the only country with the law of sedition. It may therefore, be relevant to consider whether decisions from other jurisdictions will be of value in interpreting the sections of the law on sedition. In *R.* v *Wallace Johnson*,[11] the court held that the code should be construed in its application to the facts of the case free from any glosses or interpolations derived from any expositions, however authoritative. Thus, it was held that

---

[9] (1960) FSC 251.
[10] *Supra*
[11] *Supra*

section 50 (2)(a), (b), (c) and (d) could not be said to require "intention" to excite violence or "public" disorder as in England. The defendant was charged with sedition in that he distributed a pamphlet containing a seditious publication to wit: "Down with the enemies of the people, the exploiters of the weak and oppressors of the poor: etc." The pamphlet was directed against the government of the federation. The defence submitted that sections 50 and 51 of the criminal code in so far they relate to the Government of Nigeria were inconsistent with the provision of section 24 of the Constitution of the Federation, upon the grounds that -

> any law which punishes a person for making a statement which brings a Government into discredit or ridicule, or creates disaffection against the government irrespective of whether the statement is true or false and irrespective of any repercussions on public order or security is not a law which is reasonably justifiable in a democratic society.

The prosecution submitted that those sections of the criminal code were not inconsistent with section 24 of the Constitution of the Federation and that the Fundamental right of expression was protected adequately by section 50 (2) of the criminal code in this regard. The court established the following principles in this case:

(i) in section 50 (2) of the criminal code,
  (a) the words "the Government of Nigeria as by law established," considered in the light of the Nigeria (Constitution) Order in Council, 1960 meant the body of persons who for the time being collectively exercise the authority of the Government of the Federation of Nigeria, considered as a collective

body and independently of the persons it consists of; and

(b) the words "hatred" and "contempt" meant not merely the absence of affection and regard, but disloyalty, enmity, hostility; and

(c) the word "disaffection" connotes enmity and hostility, estranged allegiance, disloyalty, hostility to constituted authority or to a particular form of political government.

(ii) It is legitimate and constitutional by means of fair argument to discuss any grievance or to criticise, canvass and censure the acts of government and their public policy; what is not permitted is to criticise the Government in a malignant manner, for such attacks, by their nature, tend to affect the public peace.

(iii) truth is no defence to a charge of sedition when the seditious intention is clear. It may, however, in certain circumstances, be a relevant consideration for the purpose of ascertaining the real intention of the person charged in considering the exceptions in section 50(2) (ii) of the code.

(iv) The purpose of subsection (3) of section 50 of the Criminal Code is to enable the prosecution to rely upon the act, or the words, or the document itself to prove intent without having to call extrinsic evidence. The subsection cannot, however, be construed so as to deprive a person of his right to show that his only intention is one of those set out in the exceptions to section 50(2).

(v) To contend that, under section 24(2) of the constitution of the Federation, a law is only valid if the acts prohibited by it are, in every case, likely to lead directly to disorder, is to take too narrow a view of the constitutional provision; for it is justifiable to take reasonable precautions to preserve public order and this may involve the prohibition of acts which, if unchecked or unrestrained, might lead to disorder, even though those acts would not themselves do so directly. The supreme court must be the arbiter of whether or not any particular law is justifiable.

(vi) On a charge of sedition, the exceptions to section 50(2) of the criminal code form a sufficient protection of the rights of freedom of expression guaranteed by section 24 of the Constitution of the Federation; and sections 50 and 51 of the Criminal Code are not invalidated by the constitutional provision.

The conclusion of the court is to the effect that Nigerian criminal code does not have the requirement of incitement to violence before a conviction for sedition can be justified on the ground that sedition is a statutory offence in Nigeria and since this requirement cannot be found in the Code, it could not be imported into it in spite of the fact that this element should be proved in England from where this offence was imported. The reason for expunging this requirement from the Criminal Code has been eloquently put by Nwabueze in his book *Constitutional Law of the Nigerian Republic* thus:

Based, as it is on Stephen's Digest of the criminal law, this definition is believed to have been specially designed to strengthen the hands of the colonial administration in dealing with possibility that a handful of educated natives might incite the gullible populace to hatred, disloyalty or violence against the Government. Because of the easy excitability of illiterate peasants and the bitter emotion which imperialism is apt to generate in the minds of colonial peoples, it was thought unnecessary that words alleged to be seditious should have a tendency to provoke violence as in the case in English law. As was anticipated, the colonial administration found it necessary to make rather ample use of the law particularly against the militant zikists of the forties.[12]

In *Service Press* v *A.G*,[13] Foster-Sutton P. held that the gist of this offence lies in the seditious intention as defined, which intention is to be gathered from the contents of the publication and that the truth of the matter published has no bearing on the character of the publication. This absolute statement was qualified in *D.P.P* v *Chike Obi*,[14] where the Supreme Court held that section 50 (3) of the Criminal code cannot be construed so as to deprive a person of his right to show that his only intention is one of those set out in the exceptions to section 50 (2) of the criminal code and for this purpose truth may be a relevant consideration.

The position of the offence of sedition under the 1979 Constitution

In *D.P.P.* v *Chike Obi*,[15] the defence contended that sections 50 and 51 of the Criminal Code were inconsistent with section 24 of the 1960 Constitution which provided for freedom of expression. Ademola FCJ held that -

---

[12] At pg. 397. D.C Holland in *Equality before the Law* (1958) 8 C.L.P. 74 at p. 87 said "the privilege of pointing out errors and defect must often be proved, since the dispassionate pointing out of errors may well excite hatred and contempt against those responsible for them. And the more grievous the error or defect, the more likely it is that hatred and contempt will be excited."

[13] (1952) 14 WACA 176.

[14] *Supra.*

[15] *Supra.*

> This is taking too narrow a view of the provision and that it
> must be justifiable in a democratic society to take reasonable
> precaution to preserve public order and this may involve the
> prohibition of facts which if unchecked and unrestrained
> might lead to disorder even though those acts would not
> themselves do so directly.[16]

The learned Judge thus concluded that the court must be the arbiter of whether or not any particular law is reasonably justifiable.

The Supreme Court of Nigeria exhibited the same frame of mind in *R.* v *Amalgamated Press*,[17] where it was held that section 24 of the 1960 Constitution relating to Fundamental Human Rights guaranteed nothing but ordered freedom and that it cannot be used as a licence to spread false news likely to cause fear and alarm to the public.

This was the position of the law until Araka C. J. (Anambra State) gave his decision in *Ivory Tower Trumpet*,[18] which questioned the constitutionality of the offence of sedition. In this case the accused persons were charged with the offence of sedition contrary to section 51(1) (a) of the Criminal Code. The prosecution alleged that the accused published an article in the *Weekly Trumpet* titled "Just Before The Battle" with the intention of bringing into hatred or contempt or of exciting disaffection against the person of the Governor of Anambra State. In the said article the Governor was accused of "keeping and spending party money without account." The prosecution said the publication was seditious and called witnesses who gave evidence to the effect that when they read the article they

---

[16] At page 196
[17] (1961) 1 All NLR 199
[18] (1983) 3 F.N.R. 60.

thought the Governor was unfit for his office. The defence counsel submitted that since the premier and the prime minister were not mentioned in section 50(2)(a) of the Criminal Code because they were politicians, a similar consideration must apply to state Government under the 1979 Constitution because they also were politicians. The defence further submitted that since section 36 of the Constitution gives everyone freedom of expression, a person cannot commit a seditious act if he speaks out against offences committed by the Governor for which he could be removed under section 170 of the Constitution or lays grounds on which charges of infringement against the code of conduct could be levelled against him.

Araka C.J. (Anambra state), after a lengthy review of the position of the law on sedition in other jurisdictions, held that to sustain the existing law on sedition the court must be satisfied that it is reasonably justifiable in a democratic society in the interests of defence, public safety, public order, public morality or public health. The only reasonable restriction being in the interests of public order or safety. He held further that as the allegation in this case could not create public disorder or that it could lead to infraction of public order or safety, it could not be sustained. The case that actually brought to public glare the position of this offence under the 1979 Constitution is the case of *Arthur Nwankwo* v *The State*.[19] In that case, Mr. Arthur Nwankwo published a booklet titled "How Jim Nwobodo Rules Anambra State" which contained serious allegations on the person and administration of the then Governor Nwobodo. He was arraigned before Nwokedi J of the High Court of Onitsha. He was convicted and sentenced to 12 months in jail and ₦50.00 fine was imposed on the two counts of publishing and distributing seditious materials. An order was also made for

---

[19] (1983) 2 F.N.R. 283.

complete withdrawal of the said book from irculation. In coming to this conclusion, the trial court placed great reliance on the earlier cases of *Chike Obi*[20] and *Service Press Ltd*,[21] among others.

The accused appealed to the Court of Appeal. The appeal touched on procedural irregularities, substantive criminal law and constitutional inconsistencies. Of particular importance was the determination of the question whether sections 50(2) and 52 which cover the law of sedition can stand in Nigeria in view of the provision of section 36 of the 1979 Constitution which provides that a citizen has the right to freedom of expression, which includes freedom to hold opinion and to receive and impart idea and information without interference, the only restriction being the provision of section 41 of the same Constitution. Section 41 of the 1979 Constitution provides *inter alia* that:

> (a) nothing in section 36 of this constitution shall invalidate any law which is reasonably justifiable in a democratic society in the interest of defence, public health or for the purpose of protecting the right and freedom of others.

It was the opinion of the trial court that the provision of the Criminal Code relating to sedition is not inconsistent with the provision of the Constitution. The court of Appeal however justifiably disagreed with the High Court decision on this issue. Belgore J.C.A. who delivered the lead judgment held that sections 50(2), 51 and 52 which cover the law of sedition are inconsistent with the provisions of sections 36 and 41 of the Constitution. The existence of the Criminal Code was however

---

[20] *Supra.*
[21] *Supra.*

not doubted by the Court of Appeal as the validity of all laws enacted before the 1979 Constitution was enacted into law has been preserved by its section 274.[22]

It is pertinent to state that the provisions of the law under section 36 and section 41 of the 1979 Constitution could be found in the 1960[23] Constitution under which the earlier decisions were reached. The Court of Appeal in stating the effect of the provision relating to freedom of expression under the 1979 Constitution as opposed to the 1960 Constitution stated that the 1960 Constitution operated during a Parliamentary system as distinct from the present system of Presidentialism where the incumbents underwent mudslinging and rigours of campaigns and rallies to win their offices. It was thus held that they could not be said to be wearing the same constitutional protective cloaks of their predecessors under the 1960 Constitution.

Olatawura J.C.A. was of the opinion that:

> the law of sedition which has derogated from freedom of speech guaranteed under this 1960 Constitution is inconsistent with the 1979 Constitution more so when this cannot lead to a public disorder as envisaged under section 41(1) (a) of the 1979 Constitution.[24]

He then remarked that: "we are no longer the illiterates or the mob society our colonial masters had in mind when the law was promulgated."[25]

---

[22] Section 274 (1) of the 1979 Constitution provides that "subject to the provisions of this constitution, an existing law shall have effect with such modifications as may be necessary to bring it into conformity with the provisions of this Constitution..."

[23] See section 24 of 1960 Constitution as well as section 25 of 1963 Constitution.

[24] at page 310

[25] Ibid.

It has been stated that the law of sedition was based on the English notion that the king or Queen could do no wrong. Earlier cases were decided when British West African colonies were subjects of the King or Queen of England. Even after independence, Nigeria, like other countries in this regard, still tried to save the sections as originally existed in Laws of Nigeria 1948 with modifications of replacing the "Queen and heirs and successors" with the President or Governor of a Region.[26]

Indeed the 1960 Constitution was based on Parliamentary system, hence the earlier decisions along the English conception of the law of sedition.[27]

With the promulgation of the 1979 Constitution, which was modelled along the American Presidential system of government,[28] the English notion of the law of sedition could not be retained. Hence, the new disposition of the courts to look at the offence of sedition from another angle. For example, there is no ban in the 1979 Constitution against publication of truth except for the provisos and security necessities embodied in appropriate sections. Thus, it could be said that the new approach of the court is premised on the socio-political pattern as well as the legal framework which could no longer allow resort to laws enacted by our colonial masters to suit their purposes.

While there were equivalent provisions of sections 36 and 41 of the 1979 Constitution in the 1960 Constitution, it has been observed that the 1979 Constitution is a "composite document, a

---

[26] This is usually the pattern of legislation in some former colonies of Britain. It is sheer judicial inertia. For example in Nigeria, there is the Law Reform Commission. This body has not made any appreciable impact in changing the laws enacted notwithstanding the fact that such laws are not in consonance with our social and cultural values.

[27] This was also the position in 1963. The 1963 Constitution of Nigeria was based on the parliamentary system of government.

[28] See First Amendment and Fourteenth Amendment to the American Constitution. See also *Dennis & Ors.* v *U.S.*, 341 U.S. 494; *New York Times* v *Sullivan* 376 U.S. 254.

distinct animal from others and must be viewed only in the light of its words and circumstances." Finding analogies from other Constitutions would thus destroy its indigenousness and it will make it sound like a gramophone and the courts looking like dogs hearing the master's voice.[29]

It should be stated that the abrogation of this offence from our criminal statute will not in anyway endanger the society as section 41 of the 1979 Constitution is wide enough to solve any mischief which this offence seeks to prevent. If a publication is false news with intent to cause fear and alarm in public, or to disturb the public peace, knowing or having reason to believe that such statement, rumour or report is false, such a person can sue and if a person feels defamed, there is the civil remedy of suing for libel or slander as well. There are also provisions in Chapter XXXIII of the Criminal Code Law as to criminal defamation.[30] The above provisions seem adequate to protect any person who may feel aggrieved that his reputation has been tarnished as a result of any false publication. To retain section 51 of the Criminal code will be tantamount to leaving a deadly weapon in the hands of those in power which could be used by a corrupt government or a tyrant.[31] Just as Olatawura J.C.A. said in this case,[32] those who occupy sensitive posts must be prepared to face public criticisms in respect of their office so as to ensure that they are accountable to the electorate. They should not be made to feel they live in an Ivory Tower and therefore belong to

---

[29] Per Belgore J.C.A. at page 293.

[30] Chapter XXXIII deals with defamation as (1) in the case of spoken words or audible sounds, the speaking of such sounds in the hearing of the person defamed or any other person; (2) in other case, the exhibiting of it in public, or causing it to be read or seen, or showing or delivering it, or causing it to be shown or delivered, with intent that it may be read or seen by the person defamed or by any other person.

[31] This possibility is high in Africa where those in power usually view any criticism as an act of sabotage.

[32] At page 309.

a different class. They must develop thick skin and where possible plug their ears with cotton wool if they feel too sensitive or irascible. They are within their constitutional rights to sue for defamation but they should not use the machinery of government to invoke criminal proceedings to gag their opponents, for if it is otherwise, the freedom of speech guaranteed by our constitution will be meaningless.

It could therefore be said that the retention of the offence of sedition in our criminal code is unnecessary.

7

Implications of the 1999 Constitution on freedom of expression and the press

With the disengagement of the Military from civil governance on May 29, 1999,[1] the 1999 Constitution was promulgated.[2] It is necessary to consider the implications of the 1999 Constitution to freedom of expression and the press.

It has to be mentioned that until the provisions of the 1999 constitution are tested in our law courts, one can only look at it (the Constitution) vis-à-vis its forerunner, that is, the 1979 Constitution. Happily, the preamble to the 1999 Constitution states *inter alia*:

> WHEREAS the Constitutional Debate Co-ordinating Committee benefited from the receipt of large volumes of memoranda from Nigerians at home and abroad and oral presentations at the public hearings at the debate centres throughout the country and the conclusions arrived threat and also at various seminars, workshops and conferences organised and was convinced that the general consensus of

---

[1] May 29, 1999 marked the end of the Transitional Period.
[2] See Constitution of the Federal Republic of Nigeria (Promulgation) Decree No. 24 of 1999.

opinion of Nigerians is the desire to retain the provisions of the 1979 Constitution of the Federal Republic of Nigeria with some amendments;

AND WHEREAS, it is necessary in accordance with the programme on transition to civil rule for the Constitution of the Federal Republic of Nigeria after necessary amendments and approval by the Provisional Ruling Council to be promulgated into a new Constitution for the Federal Republic of Nigeria in order to give the same force of law with effect from 29th May, 1999......

Having regard to the above, germane provisions of the 1999 Constitution will now be considered vis-à-vis the 1979 Constitution.[3]

The press under the constitution

Section 36 of the 1979 Constitution dealing with right to freedom of expression and the press is section 39 of the 1999 Constitution. The provisions are similar but the second paragraph of section 36(2) which is now section 39(2) has been amended to read:

> Provided that no person, other than the Government of the Federation of a State or any other person or body authorised by the President *on the fulfilment of conditions laid down by an Act of the National Assembly*, shall own, establish or operate a television or wireless broadcasting station for any purpose whatsoever.[4]

---

[3] The discussion here relates only to the innovations introduced by the 1999 Constitution with respect to the issues discussed in this book.

[4] Addition italicised.

Section 36(3)(b) of the 1979 Constitution has been amended by the 1999 Constitution to read:

> imposing restrictions upon persons holding office under the government of the Federation or of a State, members of the armed forces of the Federation or members of the Nigeria Police Force or other Government Security Service *or agencies established by law.*[5]

Section 21 of the 1979 Constitution dealing with obligations of the mass media is section 22 under the 1999 Constitution.

The chapter dealing with Fundamental Objectives and Directive Principles of State Policy under the 1999 Constitution is chapter II like the 1979 Constitution.

Section 6 of the 1999 Constitution like section 6 of the 1979 Constitution deals with judicial powers but section 6(3), (4) and (5) has been recouched in the following terms:

> (3) The courts to which this section relates, established by this Constitution for the Federation and for States, specified in subsection 5(a) to (i) of this section shall be the only superior courts of record in Nigeria; and save as otherwise prescribed by the National Assembly of a State, each court shall have all the powers of a superior court of record.
>
> (4) Nothing in the foregoing provisions of this section shall be construed as precluding -
>
> (a) The National Assembly or any House of Assembly from establishing courts, other than those to which this section relates, with subordinate jurisdiction to that of a High Court;[6]
>
> (b) the National Assembly or any House of Assembly,

---

[5] Addition italicised.

[6] This sub-section has been re-couched.

which does not require it, from abolishing any court which it has power to establish or which it has brought into being .[7]

(5) This section relates to -

   (a) the Supreme Court of Nigeria;

   (b) the court of Appeal;

   (c) the Federal High Court;

   (d) the High Court of the Federal Territory, Abuja;[8]

   (e) a High Court of a State;

   (f) the Sharia Court of Appeal of the Federal Capital Territory, Abuja;

   (g) a Sharia Court of Appeal of a State;

   (h) the Customary Court of Appeal of the Federal Capital Territory, Abuja;

   (i) a Customary Court of Appeal of a State;

   (j) such other courts as may be authorised by law to exercise jurisdiction on matters with respect to which the National Assembly may make laws; and

   (k) such other courts as may be authorised by law to exercise jurisdiction at first instance or on appeal on matters with respect to which a House of Assembly may make laws.

Section 41 of the 1979 Constitution, known as the 'restrictions on and derogation from fundamental rights' is section 45 in the 1999 Constitution. The chapter dealing with fundamental human rights under the 1999 Constitution, like the 1979 Constitution is Chapter IV.

Section 305 of the 1999 Constitution like section 265 of the 1979 Constitution deals with 'procedure for declaration of state of emergency' but with the addition in section 305(2) of the

---

[7] This sub-section has been re-couched.

[8] The courts established for the Federal Capital Territory, Abuja have been added. They are as contained in section 6(5)(d), (f) and (h).

1999 Constitution that the proclamation must include "details of the emergency" or as the sub-section states:

> 305(2) the President shall immediately, after the publication, transmit copies of the Official Gazette to the Government of the Federation containing the proclamation *including the details of the emergency* to the president of the senate and the speaker of the House of Representatives, each of whom shall forthwith convene or arrange for a meeting of the House of which he is President or Speaker, as the case may be, to consider the situation and decide whether or not to pass a resolution approving the Proclamation.

Disclosure of source of information

As stated above, section 36 of the 1979 Constitution dealing with freedom of expression and the press is now section 39 of the 1999 Constitution. The new phrases introduced to the section have been stated above.

Furthermore, as stated above, section 41 of the 1979 Constitution tagged the derogation section is now section 39 of the Constitution.

Contempt of Court

Section 33(12) of the 1979 Constitution dealing with conviction only in accordance with specifically defined law is section 36(12) of the 1999 Constitution. It states:

> Subject as otherwise provided by this Constitution, a person shall not be convicted of a criminal offence unless that

offence is defined and the penalty therefore is prescribed in a written law; and in this subsection, a written law refers to an Act of the National Assembly or a Law of a State, any subsidiary legislation or instrument under the provisions of a law.

Sedition

The discussion on section 36 of the 1979 Constitution which is now section 39 of the 1999 Constitution should be noted. The same goes for section 41 of the 1979 Constitution which now section 45 of the 1999 Constitution.

Index